THE DRAWINGS OF
JOHN
BUTLER
YEATS

January 25, 1988

Harry !

The Luck
of the "Irish" !
Congratulations on your
victory at the Board Winner
Competition !

Christie Jules

William Butler Yeats (1865-1939)
by John Butler Yeats, 1899
Catalogue no. 13

THE DRAWINGS OF
JOHN
BUTLER
YEATS
(1839-1922)

Essay and Catalogue by
FINTAN CULLEN

With a Brief Biography by
WILLIAM M. MURPHY

Foreword by
DANIEL ROBBINS

Exhibition and Catalogue
ALBANY INSTITUTE OF HISTORY & ART
and
THE DEPARTMENT OF THE ARTS,
AND THE DEPARTMENT OF ENGLISH
OF UNION COLLEGE

FRONT COVER
SELF-PORTRAIT
Pencil on paper, inscribed:
"Myself/seen through a/glass darkly/
by/JB Yeats/Oct. 1919"
Collection: William M. Murphy

THE DRAWINGS OF JOHN BUTLER YEATS
Exhibition at the Albany Institute of History & Art, April 11-May 31, 1987

Edited by William M. Murphy
Exhibition and catalogue design by Thomas Nelson
Printed and bound in an edition of 2,000 on Mohawk Superfine 80 lb. softwhite
text and cover by Lane Press of Albany, New York

*Founded in 1791, the Albany Institute of History & Art is dedicated to collecting,
preserving, interpreting, and promoting an interest in the history, art, and
culture of Albany and the Upper Hudson Valley Region. The museum achieves
this mission through its collections, exhibitions, education programs, library,
research projects, publications and other programs offered to the general public.
The Albany Institute of History and Art is accredited by the American
Association of Museums*

This exhibition and publication were made possible, in part,
with public funds from the New York State Council on the Arts.

Contents

9
Foreword
Daniel Robbins

11
John Butler Yeats: The Artist and the Man
William M. Murphy

17
"To so paint that people should, perforce, see. . ."
Fintan Cullen

31
Notes to Essay

33
Catalogue
Fintan Cullen

112
Notes to Catalogue

114
Bibliography

Lenders to the Exhibition

James Augustine Healy Collection of
Irish Literature, Colby College

Delaware Art Museum

Mr. and Mrs. J. Robert Maguire

William M. Murphy

Anne Butler Yeats

Michael Butler Yeats

Foreword

Daniel Robbins
May I. C. Baker Professor of the Arts,
Union College

This exhibition and its catalogue originated in the admiration of one Union professor for the work of another. A few years ago, in consulting a revised bibliography of John Quinn, the New York Irish-American art patron (1870-1924), I came upon *Prodigal Father: The Life of John Butler Yeats (1839-1922)*, a biography of the father of the Irish poet William Butler Yeats. I was astonished to learn that its author, William M. Murphy, was a member of the faculty at Union College in Schenectady, New York, where I had just come as Professor of the Arts. The elder Yeats was an artist, and Murphy's book contains reproductions of many of his beautiful drawings. It also contains two pieces of information that were to have a direct effect on this exhibition. In his preface Murphy disclaims any pretensions to being a critic of art and announces that his book is a biography only, "not a critique of art, JBY's or anyone else's." He goes on to say: "Perhaps this volume may provide material for others interested in digging more deeply into some of the subjects mentioned, but no final treatment . . . is attempted here." The other fact, which I found hard to believe, was that John Butler Yeats had never had an exhibition of his own in the United States.

I approached Professor Murphy about the prospect of a retrospective exhibition, and he agreed at once. We were fortunate in obtaining the complete cooperation of John Butler Yeats's two grandchildren, Anne Butler Yeats and Michael Butler Yeats, daughter and son of the poet. Their generosity has provided the bulk of the material in the exhibition, the rest coming from institutional collections like the John Sloan Collection at the University of Delaware and the James A. Healy Collection at Colby College, and from the private collections of Mr. and Mrs. J. Robert Maguire and Professor Murphy.

We were also able to secure the services of Fintan Cullen, a graduate student at Yale University whose special field of interest was (and remains) eighteenth-century British and Irish painting. The results of his thorough study over a period of more than two years of Yeats's work are embodied in the main essay and catalogue herein.

To cap our good luck, the Albany Institute of History and Art, under its now retired director, Norman Rice, and his successor, Christine Miles, agreed to be host for the opening of the exhibition. To them and to the staff of the Institute we are deeply in debt, for without their active involvement all the research and other effort put into the preparation for the show might have proved fruitless. Tom Nelson of the Institute has undertaken the difficult job of preparing the drawings for matting and framing, and coordinating the production of the catalogue. To him and to other members of the Institute who have given us of their time and energy—Mary Dickerman, Tammis Groft, Christine Robinson and Clare Weber—we express our gratitude. To Mr. John Byron, former president of the Museum Board, we give thanks for his encouragement and support. We appreciate Nina Fleishman's conscientious editing of all the copy for this project.

Exhibitions can not be mounted without financial support. We are deeply grateful to the New York State Council on the Arts for a generous grant coming at a crucial time, and to the Union College Internal Education Fund for seed money.

We also acknowledge with thanks the patience and kindness of many people who have helped make the exhibition possible, chiefly, of course, Anne and Michael Yeats, but also Mrs. Michael Yeats, who graciously endured the invasion of her home in Dublin; Mr. and Mrs. J. Robert Maguire; Helen Farr (Mrs. John) Sloan; Professor Douglas Archibald, J. Fraser Cocks III, special collections librarian, and Patience Anne Lenk, of Colby College, Waterville, Maine; Patrick Noon, curator, along with the staff of the Department of Prints and Drawings, Yale Center for British Art, New Haven, Connecticut; Ann Stewart, librarian, National Gallery of Ireland, Dublin; Alexandra Verrigni, secretary to the Arts Department at Union College, and Beth Stinson, photo technician, also of Union. Professor Murphy, who has edited the catalogue, wishes to give special thanks to Thora Girke, secretary to the English Department at Union College, who prepared most of the typescript.

John Butler Yeats: The Artist and the Man

William M. Murphy
Thomas Lamont Research Professor
of Ancient and Modern Literature,
Union College

If ever an artist needed an agent, it was John Butler Yeats. With no gift for organization and no head for business, he resisted offers of assistance from family and friends and stubbornly went his own way. The only exhibition of his works during his lifetime was arranged by a fellow artist, and even this was an exhibition shared with another painter. The only two books published over his name, separated by fifty years, were prepared for the press by other people. The first and until now only exhibition devoted solely to him was not held until fifty years after his death. Until now he has never been exhibited in the country which he adopted as his own for the last fourteen years of his life. He cared little—it would not be correct to say "nothing"—for recognition in his own lifetime, and he was cavalier about monetary rewards for honest work well done. Not until three years after setting up shop as a painter did he receive his first commission, and that from a friend who almost forced it on him. He destroyed many paintings and sketches as unsatisfactory and reworked many others after they had reached their highest point of development. He kept no record of his works and did not encourage others to do so. His daughter Lily, who worshiped him as a person and a father, summed him up well when she said that he was "headstrong, and no manager." For his reputation as an artist he was his own worst enemy.

Few men came into the world with better prospects than John Butler Yeats. He was born with a brilliant mind, a remarkable artistic talent, a healthy body (except, paradoxically for an artist, for poor eyes), and money enough to make life easy. His father, the Reverend Mr. William Butler Yeats, a clergyman in the Church of Ireland (the cousin of the Church of England, what in America we would call the Episcopal Church), was serving in the Parish of Tullylish in County Down, Ulster, when John Butler Yeats was born there on March 16, 1839. After a happy early boyhood he was sent off to a school near Liverpool and then, in his teens, to Atholl Academy on the Isle of Man, where his talents as a pencil portraitist made him popular with students and schoolmasters. He entered Trinity College, Dublin (TCD), in December of 1857 and soon found himself immersed in the intellectual currents sweeping Europe, emerging as a convinced Darwinist and a disciple of John Stuart Mill and Auguste Comte, the Positivist. Yet he felt the transforming power of art and never succumbed to a common failing of the materialists, the belief that beauty was of no importance. John

Butler Yeats was no Benthamite. He was a worshiper, and a deeply religious one, but for the God of his fathers he substituted Beauty and Truth. He fell in with three other young luminaries of TCD, John Todhunter and the Dowden brothers John and Edward, and with them he explored religion—John Dowden would soon be ordained a clergyman—and philosophy and poetry.

In 1862, on vacation in Sligo, where his grandfather John Yeats had been Rector of Drumcliff Parish, he met and fell in love with Susan Pollexfen, eldest daughter of a prosperous grain merchant and steamship owner, and sister of two of his schoolmates at Atholl Academy. Shortly after their engagement the Reverend William Butler Yeats died, and the twenty-three-year-old JBY, by this time a law student at the King's Inns, came into an estate of more than 560 acres in County Kildare and a rental house in Dublin, the whole evaluated at 10,000 pounds and bringing in annual gross rents of 500 pounds and net of 380, enough to have made him financially independent if he had known how to manage money. At law school he proved the most popular as well as the most gifted student and in November 1865 was chosen to give the annual address (later published) before the Debating Society in the presence of the most distinguished jurists and barristers in Ireland. At that moment he seemed well launched on a voyage that would carry him to the rich harbors of the Four Courts of Dublin. It is ironic to have to record that the other three of the TCD quartet, not without the gene of survival, became conventional successes in their chosen fields—Todhunter a distinguished physician and a published, if underpraised, poet; John Dowden the bishop of Edinburgh; and Edward Dowden a professor of literature at TCD and one of the world's most widely acclaimed academic critics—while John Butler Yeats never again attained the secular peak represented by his speech before the Debating Society.

For shortly afterward he made a sudden decision, and from that moment the conventional career of achievement and reward began to recede and slowly but inevitably disappeared. Dissatisfied with the emptiness of the barrister's profession and the social life that went with it, he abruptly moved to London to embark on a career as an artist. He took with him his wife, their two-year-old son Willie (William Butler Yeats), and year-old daughter Lily. Susan Pollexfen Yeats, committed to the values of her father's family, was thrown into a state of distress by her husband's quixotic maneuver, which deprived her of the fashionable life she had looked forward to as a barrister's wife in Dublin. She took no interest in her husband's work, either in the art he studied at the Heatherley and Slade Schools, or in the studies of William Blake he shared with his fellow artists J. T. Nettleship, George Wilson, and Edwin Ellis. She was terrified at the prospect of financial ruin as her husband, with no earned income and living beyond his means, gradually mortgaged his Kildare properties—and even sold the income-producing rental house in Dublin—to make ends meet. Children continued to arrive: Elizabeth Corbet ("Lollie") in 1868, John Butler, Jr. ("Jack") in 1871, and two others who died young. As expenses rose and income declined, Susan entered on a long course of mental distress that would culminate in total psychosis twenty years later.

The beginning art student, unsure of his powers, worked hard at his new vocation, practicing, experimenting, constantly tearing up or rubbing out or painting over. Friends recognized his talent and praised his work, but he was dissatisfied with it. One of the most amusing stories about him is told by his son the poet in his *Reveries Over Childhood and Youth*. JBY, practicing landscape painting at Burnham Beeches, began a painting in the spring and as the season wore on added the buds and leaves to what had been bare trees, then covered them over with the rich foliage of summer, painted the green out again as fall came, and ended up with a landscape of snow. Where another artist would have painted four pictures and sold them all, JBY painted only one and did not sell it. Practical artists save their experiments or sell them for what the market will bear. JBY, in a half century of painting, destroyed or lost or let slip away almost as much artistic wealth as he preserved. Though in an ideal world things may be otherwise, in this one success in art is measured by recognition through exhibitions and sales, but John Butler Yeats could not bring himself to master the arts of self-advertisement and salesmanship. Dante Gabriel Rossetti expressed an interest in his work and asked to meet him, but some loose bolt in JBY's psyche prevented him from accepting the invitation. Robert Browning admired JBY's **Pippa Passes** (Fig. 3) and came to offer his congratulations. But the artist was not at home and made no attempt to bring the great poet back. A relationship with Rossetti or Browning might have been worth much to the young artist, but he could not bring himself to forge one.

One difficulty that plagued John Butler Yeats from the beginning was that he possessed more than one talent. Not many good writers are also good artists; and not many artists write well. JBY regarded himself, and wanted others to regard him, as an artist, but he was also a gifted writer. And, to top his other talents, he was a brilliant speaker as well. In a time of great conversationalists he was regarded as one of the best. His letters constitute delightful essays on art, literature, and philosophy. Yet since he regarded himself as a painter, he made no effort to perfect his conversation or writing but merely struck off sparks of brilliance in each. Perfectionism he

reserved for his paintings, yet his interest in matters outside of art resulted in a diversion, and perhaps a dilution, of his talents, that may have made it impossible for him to achieve perfection in anything. He was like an Olympic athlete who chooses the pentathlon, performing brilliantly in many events while not a champion in any; and painting was only one of the many events in which he shone. He paid a price for his diversity, like the hero of Robertson Davies's novel *A Mixture of Frailties*. Giles Revelstoke is a brilliant composer who fancies himself also a writer and stage manager. His fictional critic Aspinwall writes of one of his works:

> Though musical gifts and literary skill have often gone hand in hand there comes a time when one or the other must take the lead. Mr. Revelstoke will forgive me if I point out that, as Schumann, Berlioz and Debussy in their time had to give up their avocation as writers to embrace their fate as composers, that time has also come to him. In brief, he must give up what he does well and devote himself to what he does best. (New York: Viking/Penguin, 1983, p. 227)

Like Revelstoke, JBY was perhaps not single-minded enough in doing what he did best. And he had no mind at all for business, as others did. Most artists have the sense to cultivate their reputations as well as their talents; John Butler Yeats lacked that sense completely. Oliver Elton, a professor of literature at the University of Manchester and a long-time friend and admirer, declared that JBY was "spectacularly not on the make."

The pattern established in the early London days remained unchanged throughout his life. His works were occasionally shown in exhibitions, but he was unable to profit from them. When JBY realized in the early 1870s that he was living beyond his means with no hope of improving his lot, he returned to Ireland, hoping to make his fortune there as a portrait painter. After a brief and unsuccessful stay he tried London again. He always believed success was waiting for him in a city other than the one he was living in. The second London career was no more successful than the first. By 1880, after a decade of dedicated work but still with no agent to manage his affairs, he had achieved little recognition and made little money. So once more he returned to Dublin. He did not endear himself to those of the Anglo-Irish Protestant establishment from whom he sought commissions, for he was an outspoken Irish Nationalist, a follower of Isaac Butt who believed in Home Rule, a supporter of the Celt over the Saxon. He joined the Contemporary Club, where Nationalists met to discuss their country's culture, and became one of its most celebrated members. In the ensuing years he simultaneously enjoyed the pride and suffered the humiliation of watching his older son William Butler Yeats begin his astonishing career as poet, dramatist, and Irish Nationalist and outstrip his father in productivity and influence. John Butler Yeats was of course himself responsible for much of his son's achievement, for to his roles as artist, philosopher, conversationalist and letter-writer he added that of the demanding father. It was his own insistence to his children on the supremacy of the artistic over the material that encouraged the manifestation of their own unique qualities. It is not widely realized in circles outside Anglo-Irish culture that JBY was the father not only of the Nobel-prize-winning poet, but also of the painter Jack Yeats; of the publisher of the Dun Emer and Cuala Presses, Lollie Yeats; and of the brilliant letter-writer and balance wheel of the family, Lily Yeats.

Because of his wife's evident unhappiness, it has been charged in some quarters that JBY was a poor husband. To the extent that over her objections he abandoned a promising career in law for the uncertain vocation of painter, the indictment is valid. But it is also true that he stuck with her relentlessly, holding the view—unusual in a bohemian—that marriage is a valuable institution; that he always defended her to their children; and that they in their writings have scarcely a good word to say for her. Lily has etched in acid some pages of commentary about her mother's moodiness and neurasthenia. On the whole, if the marriage was not a happy one, George Meredith's words best evaluate it: "The fault is mixed."

When in late 1886 and early 1887 JBY uprooted his family once again for another move from Dublin to London, Susan Pollexfen Yeats collapsed under the strain. She suffered from two strokes within a period of months after their arrival, was an invalid thereafter requiring constant care, grew increasingly detached from the world about her, and died in the first week of 1900 after almost thirteen years of illness.

Those thirteen years, when the family lived at Blenheim Road in Bedford Park (a residential community of artists and writers in the west of London towards Windsor), were perhaps the most distressing of JBY's life. He tells us that he abandoned serious painting during that period, a claim largely if not entirely true, and drew only sketches for religious tracts and illustrations for magazines and books. (His illustrations for the Dent edition of Defoe are the best known of these). His lands in County Kildare were sold to their tenants under a program of land reform, so he knew that after the final monthly payment in 1907 he would have no regular income from property that had been in the family for centuries. Lollie's diary from the late 1880s gives a harrowing account of the perpetual indebtedness of her father and the difficulties it imposed on other members of the family. William Butler Yeats wrote articles for Irish and Irish-American publications and, having learned a lesson from his father, insisted on payment for them. Jack studied art in London schools, married a woman with an independent income, and fled the family nest. Lily got a job with May Morris, daughter of William Morris, and learned embroidery in her shop, a skill she later put to use in the Dun Emer and Cuala Industries. Lollie wrote stories for magazines. It is not surprising that during that period John Butler Yeats, well-meaning but feckless head of the household, came close to a nervous breakdown himself.

Yet if his art had met a temporary roadblock, his other talents flourished. At Bedford Park he was one of the lights of the Calumets, a conversation club like the Contemporary in Dublin, whose members included the artists Joseph Nash and Henry Marriott Paget, the publisher Elkin Mathews, the Oxford Regius Professor of History York Powell (whose admiration for JBY was boundless), the Manchester professor Oliver Elton, the Russian anarchist Sergius Stepniac, and JBY's old friend John Todhunter. G. K. Chesterton, who married a girl from Bedford Park, first met JBY in the late nineties and was later to pronounce him one of the best conversationalists he had ever heard, a rare tribute, as Chesterton himself was regarded as one of the greatest conversationalists of his time.

The death of his wife freed JBY of a host of financial and emotional restrictions, and once again he was able to think of moving about. In 1901 he submitted paintings to the Royal Hibernian Academy Exhibition, which rejected them. Sarah Purser, a longtime friend of JBY's and herself a portrait painter, was furious at the insult, annoyed that JBY had never received the recognition she felt he deserved. So she organized and managed in that year an exhibition in Dublin of his works and those of another neglected Irish artist, Nathaniel Hone. Characteristically, he took no part in the arrangements himself. He had no record of the disposition of his paintings, and Miss Purser had to scout around to find their possessors. She alone arranged for the catalogue to which York Powell contributed the essay on John Butler Yeats. For a brief time, because of someone else's work, JBY was the talk of Dublin.

In the following year he, with his daughters (who were now partners in a new enterprise called the Dun Emer Industries and, later, the Cuala Industries), settled again in Dublin in a little house in Dundrum called Gurteen Dhas ("pretty little field"). Lollie became the publisher of books, Lily the producer of embroidered goods. Their father, with rejuvenated enthusiasm, seriously resumed the business of portrait painting. He had long since virtually abandoned all other kinds of painting, such as the landscapes of the 1870s and the dramatic works like **Pippa Passes** (Fig 3.), and now, with an Irish Renaissance about to flower in Dublin, he became one of its most productive members. He found himself a studio on Stephens Green and held court there regularly, entertaining other Dublin luminaries like Miss Purser, George Moore, George Russell ("AE"), John Millington Synge, Katharine Tynan, Lady Gregory, and, on his fateful visit to Ireland in 1904, John Quinn, the Irish-American lawyer, art collector, and advocate of things Irish. When Hugh Lane, Lady Gregory's nephew, decided to commission a series of portraits of distinguished Dubliners, he chose JBY for the task. Like a latter-day Lazarus, JBY embarked on a second life.

It was a career that perfectly suited his talent and temperament. In a letter to Rosa Butt (20 January 1917; Bodleian Library, Oxford), he wrote:

I have one distinction among portrait painters. I take great interest in the person I paint. Portrait painting with me is friendship or it might be hatred, but I must have a real personal interest in whom I paint, whereas other painters, even the very best, only think about the painting. They will tell you they are artists first and last, whereas I am a human being all the time. That's why my work is interesting, and that's my boast. I am always hoping for a portrait to paint. I hate writing and love painting.

As an epigraph for his book *Essays Irish and American* (1918), his editor chose Terence's "Homo sum; humani nihil a me alienum puto" (I am a human being, and nothing that is human is alien to me). In his brilliant commentary on *The Canterbury Tales*, John Livingston Lowes remarks of Chaucer's Prioress, the religious woman who kept pets, was fastidious about her manners, and strove to speak French with the proper accent—all things she should not have been interested in—that in her we find "the imperfect submergence of the woman in the nun." In JBY some may find the imperfect submergence of the human being in the artist.

The Lane commissions were not to herald better times, for the new painter was still the old person. JBY's adolescent disregard of sound business practice continued, perhaps nowhere better illustrated than in his handling of a portrait of Mrs. Dodgson Hamilton Madden, which he worked and reworked. Mrs. Madden died, and a long time later JBY personally delivered the portrait only to discover that on that very day Madden was escorting a new bride to his home. JBY had to do things his own way, and his way was not the way of business. He treated Lane's subjects as he treated Madden, and a frustrated Lane was compelled to ease him out as court painter and give the job to William Orpen. "Mr. Yeats does not work well in harness," Lady Gregory commented drily.

Nevertheless, the five years he spent in Dublin from 1902 to 1907 saw the production of some of his best work: the magnificent oil of John O'Leary (Fig. 2; thought by some to be his finest portrait), others of Lady Gregory, Synge, Russell, and William Butler Yeats, and scores of brilliant pencil sketches. He sketched or painted almost every person of importance in the Irish Renaissance except Maud Gonne, whom he disliked, and James Joyce, whom he scarcely knew.

Yet the lack of a business sense remained. He did not charge enough for his work and seldom insisted on payment from dilatory sitters, even those most able to pay. The world accepted him at his own evaluation, and so he achieved neither fame nor fortune. One result was that he could not contribute what he thought was his fair share to the operation of the household in Dundrum. In that house tensions mounted as Lollie, the frustrated and excitable younger daughter, grew more and more paranoid as she moved relentlessly toward nervous breakdown. Then, in March 1907, around the time of his sixty-eighth birthday, two other almost simultaneous events convinced JBY that further life in Dublin, where he felt himself a failure, was impossible. The final payment was made on his lands in County Kildare, and

John O'Leary, his old and admired friend, died. When later in the year his daughter Lily was invited to New York City to display Dun Emer's wares, JBY impulsively decided to join her. They arrived in New York during the last week of 1907. John Quinn met them there, took care of their obligations to the Customs Office, and behaved as a magnificent host, taking them everywhere and introducing them to his influential friends.

Perhaps Quinn overdid his hospitality; perhaps there were underground streams in JBY's psyche that are beyond exploring. Whatever the reasons, and JBY could never explain them himself, he put off his return to Ireland again and again until it finally became clear to him and everyone else that he had no intention of going back. Whatever the disadvantages of New York, they were nothing compared to those of Dublin. Now, in a big and fascinating metropolis that would have held a dozen Dublins, he was to go Lazarus one life better. For the fourteen years until his death in 1922 he was an enthusiastic resident of New York and America, both of which he admired beyond measure. Robert Henri, the artist, was to say that the story of JBY's flight to America was that "of an old man who ran away from home and made good." Certainly New York gave him new life and new purpose, and he turned to them with a will.

Through Quinn JBY met virtually every Irish-American of importance in New York. One day he attended a luncheon in his honor given by Francis Hackett and Whidden Grahame, with John Burroughs in attendance. In February he lectured at the Sinn Fein Club, his talk appearing as a two-column spread in *The Evening Sun*. On June 24, 1908, at a dinner at Delmonico's, he was one of Quinn's twenty-three guests, seven of them justices of the New York Supreme Court. JBY made an impromptu speech and won the instant admiration of his listeners. William Jay Gaynor, soon to become mayor of New York, praised his speech as "a gem of after-dinner speaking," and he was so impressive at the Vagabonds Club that he was named an honorary member, the first in its history. He spoke before the Friendly Sons of St. Patrick and was a guest at the homes of Judges Dowling, Byrne, and Keogh. For the first few months of his sojourn he received commissions and promises of commissions, only to suffer again, through his own habits, the same indignities as befell him in Dublin and London. He tried to be witty about his fate. "The Americans are a promising people, as I sometimes tell them," he wrote to William Butler Yeats, "without letting them know that I speak in irony."

Quinn was at that time a power in Democratic politics, attending the 1908 presidential nominating convention in Denver, where his candidate lost. Quinn was JBY's passport to the Irish in America, and if not everyone granted him a visa, it was not Quinn's fault. In fact, after the first few years in New York JBY found himself moving away from the American Irish, with whom indeed he had little in common save nationality, and whom he found decidedly inferior to their cousins in the old country. America did something to immigrants, and its effect on the Irish was not always admirable. Gradually he drifted into the company of artists and writers who were to remain his chief source of friendship in his final years.

By 1908, of course, JBY's technical facility had diminished. His handwriting, once large and flowing, had been reduced to a miniscule, almost indecipherable scrawl. George Russell thought that his eyesight, always poor, was now unable to discriminate colors accurately. His pencil sketches were increasingly done in thin scratchy lines. Yet his new environment filled him with an energy that had weakened in Dublin, and the result was many oils and hundreds of pencil portraits, most still untraced in the homes of New Yorkers. Of all the commissions given him, the one by John Quinn for a self-portrait in oils was the most amusing and melancholy—productive for JBY, maddening for Quinn. Quinn commissioned it on February 3, 1911, and when JBY died eleven years to the day later, it stood unfinished on the easel beside his deathbed. Viewing himself in a mirror, he worked at it sporadically, sometimes for long stretches of feverish intensity, sometimes for brief moments of dabbling. He scraped out countless finished versions to begin anew, yet it seems fair to conclude that he intended to leave it unfinished when he died. Even so, Quinn, whose astuteness as an art critic is legendary, wrote of it to William Butler Yeats, "If Cézanne's name had been painted to it people would say, 'What a wonderful thing it is.' " He remarked on its "wonderful richness of color, color that even Renoir never got," color "cooler than Renoir's."

In the process of working on it JBY did many pencil sketches of himself, some of the head only, some of the whole body, like the 1919 sketch which he inscribed "Myself seen through a glass darkly," one of his finest works.

Yet to Americans JBY was either not known as a painter or was accepted as one in only a secondary way, being admired primarily as a talker. When he moved into the Petitpas boardinghouse at 317 West 29th Street in 1909, a minute's walk from the Main Post Office and Pennsylvania Station, he entered a world of fellow bohemian writers and artists, men like John Sloan and Robert Henri, Van Wyck Brooks, Alan Seeger, and Conrad Aiken, women like the poet Jeanne Robert Foster and the miniaturist Eulabee Dix Becker. For the last twelve years of his life he held court at his own table there, and it became almost a requirement among the artistic set to "dine with Yeats at Petitpas." John Sloan's well-known painting, which hangs in the Corcoran Gallery in Washington, catches the spirit of those occasions, with the old white-bearded man, "his beautiful mischievous head thrown back," holding his audience spellbound (Fig. 12). Sloan regarded the old painter as a philosopher-king, and he and his friend Henri held him in high regard as an artist. During one of his trips to Europe Henri made a detour to Ireland just to see JBY's paintings at the National Gallery of Ireland and the Municipal Gallery of Dublin. "In my opinion," he wrote to Sloan, "Yeats is the greatest British portrait painter of the Victorian era." Few other Americans had the

opportunity to see his earlier paintings, and as he still, through his own willfulness, lacked the advantage of an agent, his American work was seldom seen even in New York. Henri and Sloan included him in their show at the Macbeth Gallery in 1910, but when the great Armory Exhibition was held in 1913, even though John Quinn was involved in its organization, nobody thought to ask the old painter to participate, though his son Jack was represented. JBY was only "the father of W. B. Yeats," and, to many, merely "a garrulous old man"—his own wry self-descriptions.

To Van Wyck Brooks, the American literary historian and critic, JBY was a fount of ideas and an imposing monument to artistic integrity. Conrad Aiken was so impressed by him that he put him into one of his stories. Ezra Pound, similarly taken, found a place for him in *Cantos*. Many people who disliked William Butler Yeats adored his father, and the abundant evidence of his lovability, his broad-mindedness, his infectious enthusiasm, explains the fascination he exercised on almost everyone who met him.

Through the long years in New York he carried on an almost daily correspondence with the members of his family in Dublin, as well as with many other people both in America and abroad, and his letters provide a vivid picture of the differences between life in New York and in Dublin, between American and Irish personality and behavior. Visiting Irishmen paid their respects to him: Douglas Hyde, Standish O'Grady, Lady Gregory, Mr. and Mrs. Andrew Jameson, the Abbey Players, Nora Connolly (daughter of James Connolly, one of the leaders of the Easter Rising). Roger Casement spent an evening with him at Quinn's apartment, and when Casement was captured by the English at the time of the Rising and executed for treason, JBY wrote with disgust and loathing of the excess of British injustice. Although, like most of the Irish, JBY and his family disapproved of the Easter Rising, he saw immediately what would be the effects of the British execution of Connolly, Padraic Pearse, John MacBride, and the other leaders. "So these poor fools have been executed," he wrote his daughter Lily. "The government has done the logical thing, the average thing.... And yet they have done the wrong thing. These men are now embalmed in the Irish memory, and hatred of England, which might have died out, is now revived. Kept alive in prison, Ireland would have pitied and loved and smiled at these men, knowing them to be mad fools. In the end they would have come to see that fools are the worst criminals." JBY had the wisdom to have made a good statesman; he had not the temperament.

John Butler Yeats arrived in New York late in life and could not help regarding himself as a stranger in a strange land, yet he chose it over Dublin and London, and he praised it constantly to his friends in England and Ireland. In America, for all its brawling contentiousness and lack of formality and sometimes lack of taste, he saw the hope of the future. Right up to the end, when his family and John Quinn tried desperately to get him to go back to Ireland, he evaded them cleverly, with stubborn resolution. When he died in the room at West 29th Street on February 3, 1922, with John Quinn and Mrs. Jeanne Robert Foster watching over him in his last days, it was as a thoroughly transplanted American. His family wisely declined to have his body returned to Ireland. Appropriately, he is buried in a part of Mrs. Foster's family plot in the Rural Cemetery in Chestertown, New York, just an hour's drive north of Albany.

To the end he could not bring himself to admit that anything was "finished," either his paintings or his ideas. John Butler Yeats, whom John Todhunter called the only man he "ever really worshiped" and whom Edward Dowden described as a "genius," was always in the process of "becoming." Not only did he not take part in the publication of the two books that appeared over his name during his lifetime (not including the two Cuala selections from his letters, though he didn't oversee them either), he positively objected to the publication of the second, for he thought the essays in it not ready to be published. John Quinn authorized the old man to write his memoirs, for which he would pay him five dollars for every thousand words, but JBY fiddled and dawdled, never completing them, and they were published posthumously only after ruthless editing by his son the poet.

For a long biography of John Butler Yeats I chose the title *Prodigal Father* (Cornell University Press, 1978). *Unfinished Portrait* might have been just as apt. Perhaps the most revealing comment John Butler Yeats made about art was in a letter to William Butler Yeats in 1906: "I think every work of art should <u>survive</u> after all the labour bestowed upon it, and <u>survive as a sketch</u>. To the last it must be something struck off at a first heat." And the artist had to be "like a hawk," as he wrote in another letter, "long circling and hovering before it pounces." Sometimes JBY seemed like a hawk who never pounced at all, always seeking the perfect quarry but never finding it. In his intellectual activities he may have contributed little that was new to philosophy or political science, but he always showed a fascinating mind at work. Perhaps in his art he was the same, never—or seldom—achieving perfection, but always moving toward it, and moving with excitement and enthusiasm. He was, above all, the artist at work, and always the artist of humanity.

"To so paint that people should, perforce, see. . ."

Fintan Cullen

My father began life a Pre-Raphaelite painter; when past thirty he fell under the influence of contemporary French painting. Instead of finishing a picture one square inch at a time, he kept all fluid, every detail dependent upon every other, and remained a poor man to the end of his life . . .
W. B. Yeats, Autobiographies

It is unfortunate that for so long John Butler Yeats has been referred to as "the father of the poet" and not as "the artist" or "the portrait painter." The identification with his more illustrious son has been emphasized by the fact that on the few occasions when JBY's portraits have been exhibited, they have been used chiefly as an illustrative guide to the leaders of the Irish Literary Revival. Yet the work that led to his becoming unofficial recorder of those exciting times has received scant attention. J. B. Yeats's artistic development stretched from his student days in the 1860s and 1870s, when he was a disciple of late Pre-Raphaelitism, through the 1880s and 1890s, when he developed a growing admiration for the work of George Frederic Watts and James McNeill Whistler, to his final years in New York, when he became friends with John Sloan and other members of the Ash-Can Group.

In Ireland JBY is best known as an artist for the oils that hang in the National Gallery of Ireland and in the foyer of Dublin's Abbey Theater. In the Gallery are portraits of the old Fenian John O'Leary, George Russell (AE), Douglas Hyde, and the artist's children, in the Abbey portraits of founders and players of the theater. But of the artist's drawings, his genre paintings in oils, and his work as an illustrator almost nothing has been written. Perhaps through the present exhibition John Butler Yeats will begin to receive the critical attention he deserves but failed to achieve in his lifetime and in the sixty-five years since his death.

Limited as this exhibition is to a display of, chiefly, JBY's black-and-white drawings, the viewer should not suppose that he will be seeing only the minor works of the artist. It is clear that the drawings have a power and vibrancy of their own and a consistency of quality often lacking in the oils. There are of course many fine oils, such as the 1901 portrait of Lily Yeats in the National Gallery of Ireland (Fig. 1) and that of John O'Leary (Fig. 2), but many of the paintings are victims of what the artist himself termed his "imperfect technique." JBY had a tendency, as Professor Murphy has mentioned in his essay in this catalogue, to overwork paintings and never be quite satisfied with what he had produced. His repainting of a face, hands, or posture often resulted in his ruining a perfectly good day's work; but he was his own master and no amount of pleading could make him alter his habits.

The emphasis in any portrait in the academic tradition should of course be on the eyes and the face, and also possibly the hands. JBY understood this, and in his mature works (i.e., after the mid-1890s) many of his oils are studies of flesh tones contrasted with dark sketchy backgrounds that vaguely convey the sitter's clothing or the chair on which he or she is sitting. His interest in such aspects is equally evident in the pencil drawings, which in many respects show us the real Yeats at work. Executed rapidly, the drawings capture the artist's initial idea. Through the spontaneity of his creation Yeats is able to offer us excellent likenesses, which provide not only great visual delight but surprising psychological insight as well.

Fig. 1. JBY, *Portrait of Lily Yeats,* c. 1901, oil on canvas; National Gallery of Ireland, Dublin. 35½ x 32 inches. 90.17 x 81.28 cms.

Fig. 2. JBY, *John O'Leary,* 1904, oil on canvas; National Gallery of Ireland, Dublin. 43¾ x 33⅞ inches. 111.12 x 86.36 cms.

At heart JBY was a Victorian gentleman who advocated the pursuit of the amateur over that of the professional, and, as Denis Donoghue has pointed out, it is in this light that JBY's "drawings and sketches are more successful than his paintings because they catch the gist of the matter, they encourage speed and nonchalance, and the artist was not under oath to fill up all the spaces."[1] Although he "chased," as he wrote, "the chimera of success,"[2] JBY did not approve of "a man . . . wholly occupied in getting on."[3] When WBY thought of accepting a job on a newspaper, his father was troubled by the possible effect on the poet's artistic independence. When WBY declined the offer, his father wrote to him, "You have taken a great weight off my mind."[4] He felt one had to choose between living and making a living. JBY chose living.

The critical writings about JBY as an artist are limited and unimpressive. Although he exhibited at both the Royal Academy in London (in 1887 and 1889) and the Royal Hibernian Academy in Dublin (regularly from 1880 to 1908), he never received intense or prolonged critical attention. It was not until 1901, when he was over sixty years of age, that an important retrospective exhibition of his works was held in Dublin and Yeats was allowed to enjoy the acclaim due to an artist of his maturity and quality.[5] The reviewer for *The Irish Times* spoke of Yeats's "preoccupation with character," and also, apparently in admiration, of his "difficult and laboured execution, so unlike the dash and showiness of Mr. Sargent's followers."[6] In 1924 the art historian Thomas Bodkin isolated Yeats's major quality as a "bent for the intellectual rather than the sensuous."[7] Bodkin claimed that Yeats's portraits of O'Leary, Standish O'Grady, AE, and J. M. Synge "have an air of mingled intimacy and dignity that no other portrait painter of modern time surpasses." Bodkin may be more enthusiastic than other critics, but the "intimacy and dignity" of many of the drawings are qualities specific to Yeats that dominate his work regardless of the literary fame of his sitters. Because Yeats was, as *The Irish Times* pointed out in 1901, "fortunate in having as his sitters so many distinguished and interesting personages," viewers tend to assume that the subjects are superior to the painter of them; but the intimacy of such works as the sketch portraits of Jenny Mitchell (no. 20) or "Cuckoo" York Powell (no. 21) is conveyed with such strength of execution that it is clear that the relative obscurity of the sitter makes little or no difference to our appreciation.

Subsequent discussion of Yeats's art has been scant and uninspired. His portraits and sketches of WBY are frequently reproduced in volumes on or by the poet. The 1965 centenary of the poet was marked by exhibitions that included numerous works by the father, but again he was never discussed as an artist but merely listed as the painter of portraits of his son and his son's acquaintances.[8] It was not until 1972, on the fiftieth anniversary of his death, that Yeats was given his first extensive showing since the retrospective of 1901. Displaying as it did thirty-one works, both oils and drawings, the exhibition, *John Butler Yeats and the Irish Renaissance,*[9] mounted at the National Gallery of Ireland,

provided an opportunity for a review of the career of an important Irish artist, yet it resulted in nothing but a summation of all that had gone before. By placing JBY firmly within the framework of the Literary Revival and more particularly within the shadow of his son, the exhibition failed to discuss the nature of JBY's art, the impulses behind his paintings and drawings, the details of his artistic background, and more surprisingly, given the title of the exhibition, his position as unofficial artist to this so-called Renaissance.

The publication in 1978 of William M. Murphy's encyclopedic *Prodigal Father: The Life of John Butler Yeats (1839-1922)*[10] allowed one, equipped with the essential facts for the first time, to trace the development of the artist. It is hoped that this exhibition will go some way towards introducing JBY's art to a wider audience. By placing him within the artistic context of his day it may allow us to understand more fully the varied and intriguing career of a neglected artist.

The course of Irish painting in the nineteenth century, as in the eighteenth, is closely linked with artistic movements in Britain, particularly those in London.[11] A stylistic and thematic study of the art of John Butler Yeats must necessarily be undertaken in the context of the visual arts in London from the mid-1860s to the end of the century. Dublin, although the second city of the United Kingdom, offered little to an artist eager to keep abreast of new ideas. It is necessary to remember that although JBY can be considered the most consistently rewarding and challenging Irish portrait painter of the turn of the century, he in fact spent much of his life out of the country. From 1867, when he decided to become an artist and left Dublin for London, until 1907, when he made his final move to New York, JBY spent only twelve years in Ireland.

One of the artist's earliest known works is a pen study of the landscape at Enniscrone in County Sligo, where he and his family spent the summer of 1866 (no. 1). Slightly more than half a year later Yeats abandoned the law and moved to London, where he enrolled at Heatherley's Art School. Within months of his arrival JBY was submitting ink drawings to magazines and illustrated journals from which, after a slow start, he received a small extra income.[12] The Sligo drawing, with its emphasis on line and its picturesque subject matter, may have been the kind of thing that Yeats worked up for publication in magazines like *Fun*, which is known to have accepted some of his drawings, though a thorough search of *Fun* has failed to uncover any cartoon that can be positively identified as JBY's.

At Heatherley's Art School Yeats met fellow artists like Edwin J. Ellis, John T. Nettleship, Sydney Hall, and, later, George Wilson, who together formed an informal association called "The Brotherhood."[13] The name implies a group strongly influenced by the Pre-Raphaelite Brotherhood, yet love of poetry and intellectual discussion was the main interest of its members. As Murphy has pointed out, "There was more talk of William Blake, the evangel of the Brotherhood, than the practice of painting."[14] Of the few known works by members of the group, the most dramatic must be Nettleship's extraordinary drawing **God with Eyes Turned Inward Upon His Own Glory** (c. 1869) and his equally odd illustrations for a book of poems by Arthur W. E. O'Shaughnessy.[15] The strong Blakean tone of these efforts seems to have been prevalent in two now lost drawings by JBY which he described in a letter of January 1869: one based on a scene from Browning's *In a Gondola*, the other from the Book of Job. Yeats writes of how in the second he wished to capture the moment when "Job's wife says to him 'Dost thou now retain thine integrity—curse God and die.' I have made her a large strong woman with chin thrust out, her features writhed with scorn and passion. She is of course middle aged, which makes her wild rage more terrible. Tears are slowly following each other down her cheeks. This last is the part I care for. . . ."[16]

In the early work that has survived, the influence of Blake seems to have been soon replaced by that of the contemporary Dante Gabriel Rossetti (1828-82) and others of his school. A watercolor entitled **Pippa Passes** (1869-72; National Gallery of Ireland), begun by JBY while still a student at Heatherley's, displays a desire to emulate the precision and brightly lit exactitude of the Pre-Raphaelites (Fig. 3). **Pippa** was painted under commission from Yeats's friend John Todhunter.[17] Based on Browning's poem of 1841, it shows the heroine singing her way through the countryside around Asolo in the Veneto. As she passes various groups of people, Pippa's song turns evil to good. When exhibited in Dublin in 1873 the catalogue carried the following lines from the poem:[18]

But let the sun shine! Wherefore repine?
—With thee to lead me, O Day of mine,
Down the grass path grey with dew,
Under the pine wood, blind with boughs,
Where the swallow never flew
Nor yet cicala dared carouse—
No, dared carouse!

A watercolor not eligible for inclusion in this exhibition, **Pippa Passes** displays an attention to line and flowing contour, as well as a Rossettian sense of drama and an interest in soulful young women, their mouths agape, in costumes of finely detailed exoticism. The swinging movement of the girl's apron, waistband and hair is echoed in the twisted trunks of the pine trees. The drawing was exhibited in the Dudley Gallery in London in early January 1871, and Rossetti himself is reported to have been impressed. Yet the **Pippa**, although showing obvious Rossettian qualities, may have derived them from the works of Frederick Sandys, a close follower of Rossetti, whose work is dominated by images of

Fig. 3. JBY, *Pippa Passes*, 1869-72, watercolor and mixed media; National Gallery of Ireland, Dublin. 18¾ x 13½ inches. 47.62 x 34.29 cms.

Fig. 4. Frederick Sandys, *Danaë in the Brazen Chamber*, engraving by Swain, 1867. The British Museum, London. 7 x 4 9/16 inches. 17.75 x 11.5 cms.

monumental young women.[19] In June 1868, JBY had visited Sandys, who praised the Irishman's pictures "very warmly" and encouraged him to return whenever he wanted.[20] The following January Yeats was still seeing Sandys and one afternoon spent three hours with him in his studio. They discussed art and Sandys's work, Yeats concluding that over it "there was a kind of splendid melancholy."[21] It is possible that Yeats saw Sandys's **Danaë in the Brazen Chamber**, a work of 1867 (Fig. 4), during his visits to Sandys's studio. **Pippa Passes** was begun some two years after the **Danaë** and has close compositional affinities to Sandys's piece.

Although the recipient of frequent high praise, Yeats was pathologically incapable of satisfying himself about his own creations. Todhunter had commissioned **Pippa** in 1869, but had to wait three years before receiving it. Its final delivery in April 1872 was a year after its public exhibition at the Dudley Gallery, a year, needless to add, of continuous reworkings. During the early 1870s Yeats was preoccupied with the mastering of "skill" in his art: "Possess skill and you possess money," he told his wife, whose interests lay more in the latter than the former, "and great skill means a great deal of money."[22] His friend Nettleship on one occasion referred to Yeats's "lust for perfection."[23] Unfortunately the "lust" was to lead to much frustration for himself and his family.

While still working on **Pippa** and very little else, JBY left Heatherley's for the Slade School of Art, where he attended the classes of Edward Poynter (1836-1919). Yeats spent approximately a year under his tuition (mid-1872 to mid-1873) and began practicing the artist's method of drawing and painting directly from the figure. Poynter had a "severely neoclassical bias" tinged with a decorative element that is visible in his portraits of the 1860s and 1870s.[24] His works and his teaching show a strong use of line and a feeling for the greater accessibility of the figure. He also displayed a free use of tone and showed respect for the flat surface of the canvas, thus allowing for decorative patterning effects and for a conspicuous emphasis on the use of the profile. It may be that a preoccupation with the strengthening of linearity in his drawings led to the excessive delay in Yeats's supplying Todhunter with **Pippa**, yet since all his life he failed to meet deadlines, the cause was probably more psychological than technical.

As a teacher and artist Poynter was introducing new ideas, not only to JBY but to the London art world in general. Although today we are blinded by his wholly academic style, Poynter had been one of the so-called Paris gang which had surrounded the young American James McNeill Whistler (1834-1903) in Paris during the late 1850s and early 1860s.[25] Back in London as chief instructor at the Slade from 1871 to 1876, Poynter introduced new methods which were of great interest to the young JBY:

> At Poynter's I am getting on so well that I don't like leaving it. I will tell you his method of painting which he has brought from the French Schools. Each part must be finished at once the first painting and never retouched. The whole painting must be done bit by bit.... I feel myself to be improving greatly.[26]

So by the mid-1870s Yeats had experienced a combination of influences ranging from Blake through Rossetti and Sandys to Poynter. By introducing him to the startling visual innovations of the avant-garde in Paris and London, Poynter can be credited, albeit indirectly, with greatly enlarging JBY's pictorial horizons. The pencil sketches of JBY's family and friends of the early 1870s (in particular, nos. 4 through 9) display a sensitivity to Rossetti's curvilinear softness, particularly as expressed in the latter's numerous drawings of his invalid wife Elizabeth Siddall done during the 1850s and 1860s.[27] The Yeats drawings have a delicacy and an exactitude in execution that recall Rossetti, but he adds a heavier line and shows a greater concern with the naturalness of his image than is evident in the Pre-Raphaelite. This greater naturalism, as in the drawing **William Butler Yeats as a Boy** (no. 6), is conveyed through an emphasis on tone and dark values. The sketch is finely modelled. The patterning effects of the artist's Pre-Raphaelite background have been curtailed, and Yeats has concentrated on the spontaneous capturing of a boy momentarily lost in his own thoughts.

While attending Poynter's classes Yeats may also have availed himself of the opportunity to visit Durand Ruel's London Gallery, where from 1872 to 1875 works by Manet and Degas and the Impressionists were exhibited annually.[28] The works of Henri Fantin-Latour (1836-1904) could also be seen in London after 1862, and from 1871 on were exhibited regularly at the Dudley Gallery, where JBY's **Pippa Passes** had been shown in January 1871.[29] Fantin's abstract grey backgrounds, his faithfulness to visible reality, an emphasis like Poynter's on direct painting from the model onto the canvas, may have struck Yeats as exciting new ideas and may lie behind the heightened naturalism that appears in his drawings of the early 1890s.

Like his friend Manet, Fantin frequently used his family and friends as subjects for his studies from nature. These were then worked up into paintings or etched or lithographed. Fantin's intimate subject matter (invariably women) is frequently devoid of any narrative content. Similarly, from the 1870s onward Yeats's pencil sketches are at their best when he draws those closest to him, particularly his children. There is often a feeling of solitude in his drawings, especially in those of women, more particularly those of his daughters. The solitary intimacy of such works as **William Butler Yeats as a Boy** (no. 6) and later **Lily Yeats Reclining** (no. 19) and **A Woman Dozing** (no. 22) is a definite link between JBY and the anti-anecdotal aspect of the new portraiture. Whistler, who had moved to London from Paris in the 1860s, made his most important contribution to the new trend in portraiture in the 1871 portrait of his mother, **Arrangement in Grey and Black**. It is conceivable, though no proof is presently available, that Yeats would have known of the transplanted Whistler set in London from the mid 1860s through the 1870s. It included Charles Keene (see no. 2), the printmakers Seymour Haden and Edward Edwards, Alphonse Legros, and, more peripherally, Manet and Francois Bonvin.[30]

Inspired by Poynter's enthusiasm for the works of Whistler and the new ideas emanating from France, Yeats in the early 1870s attempted to rid himself of what he called the "sensuous" world of Rossetti and his school. "I have no joy in the sensuous," he wrote in 1869, "but passion whether of love or hatred, whether what the world calls virtuous or vicious, gives me strength and is to me always a good thing. Passion is joyous, simple and strenuous. Sensuousness is melancholy and being leisurely while passion is always in great haste fond of subtleties—passion is ardent and has all its schemes in the future. Sensuousness finds food for its idle sadness in the past. To sensuousness self is everything. To passion it is nothing...."[31] Thomas Bodkin commented on the avoidance of the sensuous in Yeats's drawings and asserted that his "bent [was] for the intellectual."[32] As the years passed, the artist realized that his talent was best expressed in portraiture. A preoccupation with the mood of his sitters, combined with a newly developed concern for naturalism, began to dominate Yeats's work. In many ways, Whistler is the permanent artistic force behind the Irishman's draftsmanship, but in the 1880s his influence was matched by that of George Frederic Watts (1817-1904) and his portraits of Victorian patriarchs. Although Yeats could indicate an affinity for the naturalness and striking honesty of a portrait by Manet or Fantin, yet as a man with deeply rooted philosophical and poetic leanings his attraction to Watts's allegorical and mythological work is understandable. JBY was Watts's diligent pupil for years, and in 1906, two years after Watts's death, was invited to give a lecture on him for a major memorial exhibition in Dublin of the artist's work.[33] JBY called Watts "the greatest figure painter England has ever produced."[34] What he admired was the artist's monumentality, his Michelangelesque classicism and the timeless abstraction of his subjects. Such themes as birth, death, love, and life were of profound interest to Yeats (as they are to most of us), yet in the lecture of 1906 it was Watts's portraits that JBY singled out for special praise. From the 1850s to the end of the century Watts had been involved in what he called his Hall of Fame, a vast collection of portraits of the leading Victorians. JBY was greatly impressed by the portraits of such luminaries as Carlyle, Tennyson, and Ruskin, and observed that "the genius of portrait painting is largely a genius for friendship, at any rate I am quite sure that the best portraits will be painted where the relation of the sitter and the painter is one of friendship. . . ."[35] In 1906, when Yeats wrote these words, he was only too aware of the satisfaction to be derived from the painting of portraits of friends and of people he admired, for at that time he was busy painting portraits of some of the leading figures of the Irish Literary Revival. Equally, as the present exhibition of drawings and sketches only too clearly demonstrates, much of JBY's output over five decades was of portraits of those close to him either through family or intellectual ties. But in the context of his

lecture in 1906 it is clear that Yeats wished to acknowledge the primacy of Watts's influence on his own works. Yeats describes the "technique of portrait painting [as] mainly a technique of interpretation; to get to the colour, to model the face adequately, this to the practical hand is comparatively easy; to so paint that people should, perforce, see the particular shape of brow or eye that interest the painter, here is the true difficulty, here the true enjoyment and exquisite triumph of the painter."[36]

"To so paint that people should, perforce, see . . . ." This to Yeats was Watts's greatest legacy to the art of portraiture. Yeats's 1907 portrait in oils of John O'Leary (Fig. 2) and the pencil sketch included in this exhibition (no. 25) perfectly reflect Yeats's debt to Watts and to the latter's concern for capturing the forceful personality of a particular sitter, with slight interest in the physical details of body and surroundings. JBY's interest in Watts's patriarchal portraits seems to have begun in the early 1880s and is evident in sketches of members of Dublin's Contemporary Club (nos. 11 and 12). These quickly executed drawings display the strength of character of the subjects that is conveyed in the loose technique, the fuzzy undefined edges. A drawing of William Morris (no. 11) is as sympathetic in execution as Watts's portrait of 1870 (National Portrait Gallery, London). In Yeats's sketch Morris's full face and staring eyes are depicted in detail, in contrast to the torso and arms, which are loosely pencilled—a style that JBY was to perfect over the following three decades. Although Yeats spoke with great admiration of Watts's dedication to the revival of a classical monumentality and to subjects of strength and movement, it is understandable that he should speak more eloquently of that artist's portraiture. Yeats was only too conscious of the limitations of his own artistic talents (perhaps more conscious than he should have been), and never attempted the grandiose themes that Watts felt compelled to execute. The Irishman greatly respected Watts's remarkable individuality and artistic integrity and, on a less exalted scale, attempted to follow him in portraying man's capacity for intellectual activity.

Struggling to achieve recognition as a portrait painter, Yeats in the last decades of the nineteenth century found it extremely difficult to support himself and his family by depending on his inherited income. By the late 1880s and throughout the 1890s he was compelled to seek work actively as a magazine and book illustrator. An early drawing of this period is one that accompanied a poem by the then twenty-two-year-old WBY. The illustration to "King Goll," the tale of a mad Irish king who finds a broken harp, appeared in the magazine *Leisure Hour* in 1887 (Fig. 5).[37] The image of King Goll somewhat resembles a then celebrated painting of Hope (Fig. 6) by Watts, which was painted in 1886 and exhibited in the same year at the Royal Academy, where JBY may well have seen it. Watts's Hope is a blinded, lonely, and melancholic figure shown playing her broken lyre, which has but one taut string. Julia Cartwright, a devoted follower of Watts, writing of this painting in 1896, describes Hope as trying "with passionate longing, to catch the faint sound of the music for which she yearns."[38] In the final stanza of W. B. Yeats's "The Madness of King Goll," the wandering king tells us that while playing an "old tympan,"

> I sang how, when day's toil is done,
> Orchil shakes out her long dark hair
> That hides away the dying sun
> And sheds faint odours through the air:
> When my hand passed from wire to wire
> It quenched, with sound like falling dew,
> The whirling and the wandering fire;
> But lift a mournful ulalu,
> For the kind wires are torn and still,
> And I must wander wood and hill
> Through summer's heat and winter's cold.
> They will not hush, the leaves a-flutter round me,
>   the beech leaves old.

Mention has been made of Yeats's awareness of his own artistic limitations in the face of Watts's ambitious subject matter. Yet the sketch of King Goll, now known only through its reproduction in the pages of *Leisure Hour*, can be seen as an irregular experiment in allegorical subject matter. While Watts's allegory is of humanity clinging to the last cord of hope, Yeats appropriates the details of Watts's painting to depict the depths of mad despair and provide us with an image of his son's youthful melancholy. The drawing of King Goll increases greatly in interest when we compare it with a wash drawing of WBY dating from within a couple of years of the magazine illustration (no. 13). The dashingly bearded young poet of 1889 is the obvious model for the Irish king who destroys an old Irish harp.

The artist's use of his son as a model for an illustration to one of the latter's poems is an interesting instance of the father's identifying WBY with the subject of his poem. In later illustrative work, probably to cut expenses, JBY made extensive use of the services of his daughters, Lily and Lollie, as models for the innumerable heroines who appeared in the serialized romances in weekly magazines or in illustrations to the Dent edition of the works of Daniel Defoe. Lily Yeats was the artist's most constant companion from the 1890s until their parting in 1908 in New York City. Lily seems to have been a particularly patient model, as well as being the one who delivered the finished drawings to the offices of magazine and book publishers. As one flicks through the pages of Yeats's sketch books (no. 15), particularly those of the 1890s, one quickly becomes aware of Yeats's heavy dependence on Lily. Her form and face constantly reappear and, as with his use of WBY to illustrate the despair of King Goll, one cannot help but speculate whether JBY did not occasionally see his daughter Lily, her life largely dedicated to taking care of her father, as the perfect model for the frequently virtuous yet hapless heroines of tales he was required to illustrate.

Fig. 5. JBY, *King Goll*, *Leisure Hour*, vol. 36, 1887, p. 637.

Fig. 6. George Frederick Watts, *Hope*, 1886, oil on canvas; Tate Gallery, London. 56 x 44 inches. 160.5 x 125.5 cms.

Yeats's illustrations have received less attention than the rest of his work. They are quite considerable in number and extend from the 1860s to the 1890s. Although the artist did not enjoy producing them, his illustrative drawings reveal a talent for narrative, and, in technique, a sensitivity to wash and gouache, which he came to use regularly in the 1880s and later. During these years Yeats was a regular contributor to *Leisure Hour, Atalanta, Chum, Good Words*, and *Once a Week*, all family-oriented magazines. Most of his contributions were illustrations to trite, sentimental stories. One such tale is Frederick Langbridge's "The Dreams of Dania," a rambling melodrama of an Irish country rector and his poet-daughter, serialized in six issues of the *Leisure Hour* of 1896.[39] Lily Yeats posed for the figure of Dania and for many other of the female characters in the story. She was, to name a few, the loving daughter, the soulful poetess, and the victim of a painful romantic attachment. In "The Dreams of Dania" Yeats was illustrating a story set in Ireland and was able to incorporate a feeling for the landscape and its inhabitants which raises the sketches above the level of mere hack work. A drawing such as **An Apparition by the Wayside** (Fig. 7), through the richness of the wash and the subtlety of the lighting, conveys the damp, temperate climate of the west of Ireland. Subsequent work, such as the drawings for the Defoe commission of 1895 (Fig. 8), displays an expert knowledge of dramatic lighting effects together with a knack for capturing the telling moment. Commissioned by the publisher J. M. Dent, the Defoe drawings were to be forty-eight in number, three in each of the sixteen volumes of the complete works.[40]

Unfortunately Yeats's original small black-and-white wash drawings for the Defoe commission have been lost. The published illustrations, such as the frontispiece to *A Journal of the Plague Year* (Fig. 8)[41] are masterful exercises in tonal values, their soft lyricism most effectively captured by the then recently improved technique of photomechanical reproduction. Earlier in the nineteenth century illustration had been largely limited to wood engraving (see no. 2), but in the late 1880s and 1890s artists were able to have their designs reproduced very nearly in facsimile. Tone drawings could be reproduced by photographing the illustration through a glass screen with, as James Thorpe describes them in his book *English Illustration: The Nineties*, "fine lines of varying mesh drawn across in both directions. These break up the design into a collection of dots of varying degrees of size and closeness, thus producing a close approximation to the gradations of tone in the original."[42] An example of Yeats's prowess as an illustrator in half-tones is the so-called **Haunted Chamber** of about 1899 (no. 14). Here Yeats, to increase the effectiveness of the reproduction, has darkened the image far more than he would have in a pen drawing, the dark field being broken by two sharp accents of light. Some commentators have referred to highly tonal drawings such as this as "manière noire,"[43] a style that was immensely popular in the 1890s.

Fig. 7. JBY, *An Apparition by the Wayside*, from "The Dreams of Dania," *Leisure Hour*, vol. 45, 1896, p. 178.

Fig. 8. JBY, *Nobody stirred or answered, neither could be bear any noise*, frontispiece to *A Journal of the Plague Year*, by Daniel Defoe, vol. ix in J. M. Dent's publication of the *Romances and Narratives by Daniel Defoe*, 1895.

An element of sentiment is noticeably present in much of Yeats's illustrative work. Because of the silliness of such stories as "The Dreams of Dania," it may be possible to excuse the artist's somewhat melodramatic tendencies in the pages of *Leisure Hour*. Yet a tendency toward a certain sweetness of feeling is discernible in all his works, be it in the dependence on curved form in the charming early drawing of the young Jack Yeats (no. 7), or in the more sophisticated oil painting of 1886, **The Bird Market** (Fig. 9). Yeats often inclined towards pathos when depicting children, and yet the intent expressions on the faces of the children in **The Bird Market** deprives the work of the excessive prettiness so common to late nineteenth-century English painting of children. From the composed solitariness of **William Butler Yeats as a Boy** (no. 6, early 1870s) to the less finished but no less completely realized image of childhood introversion of the 1890s, such as the exquisite sketch of "Cuckoo" York Powell (no. 21), Yeats displays a respect for children which, even if his drawings include a tinge of sentiment, it is never maudlin but forever charming and frequently surprisingly full of insight.

Fig. 9. JBY, *The Bird Market*, c. 1886, oil on canvas; Hugh Lane Municipal Gallery of Modern Art, Dublin. 25 x 19 inches. 72.5 x 47.6 cms.

Brief mention has been made of JBY's knowledge of contemporary French art and his attraction to the naturalism of the work of Fantin and Whistler. As the century came to a close, Yeats continued to admire these two artists and was eager to associate himself with what he thought were the latest trends in western European art. His drawings of the period (1890s-1907) display a confidence of technique and purpose. His use of the tonalities of Fantin and Whistler creates a series of penetrating studies of the artist's family and close friends. A sheet such as **Lily Yeats Reclining** (no. 19) of c. 1897 boldly exploits the fidelity to nature that had been the hallmark of Fantin's numerous images of his two sisters produced during the 1860s and 1870s. Equally, Yeats acknowledges a debt to Whistler in the sketchily drawn lighting effects and the tendency to leave extensive areas of the image unfinished. In a letter of 1904, JBY referred to his work of this period as "modern and impressionist."[44] Modern they certainly are, for in the context of his letter Yeats was comparing his work with that of his younger Irish contemporary William Orpen (1878-1931), whose style the artist claimed was "learned and like an old master." In his concentrating more on naturalistic effects and less on technical bravura, Yeats by 1900 was certainly justified in his opinion that his work was up to date; yet the drawings of this period are, of course, not truly impressionist. In the first place, they do not deal with a radically new subject matter, as do the paintings of the French artists of the 1870s; further, they do not explore pure color or the dissolution of light as do those of Monet or Pissarro. To Yeats impressionism was an ensemble of tone rather than a pattern of lines and tints. The French influence in London from the 1870s onward (be it realist, naturalist or impressionist) caused a lightening of the palette, a loosening of brush strokes, in short a new diversity of technique.[45] Yeats's use of the term "impressionism" was a result of his admiration for such artists as Whistler, Fantin, and Manet; his attention to tonality in brushwork and pencilwork had been in evidence from the time of the early drawing of his son (no. 6). Now in the 1890s he developed the technique into what proved to be his most satisfying style. It is a period in which he produced far more work than in previous decades and which led to his finally becoming recognized as a major portrait painter in his native Dublin.

Yeats's use or misuse of the term "impressionism" was related to the conversation and writings of one of London's leading art critics, R. A. M. Stevenson (1847-1900). Writing for the *Pall Mall Gazette*, Stevenson strongly supported the Impressionists and their successors, both French and English. He himself had gone to Paris to study as a painter and had worked in the studio of Carolus-Duran (1837-1917) in the 1890s. While a student he had learned Duran's method of direct painting, a method much valued also by Whistler and John Singer Sargent. After failing to make his way as an artist, Stevenson returned to London and took up art journalism. During the early 1890s Stevenson visited Yeats in Bedford Park. The artist who had experimented with Poynter's and

Whistler's tonal approach and the critic who was advocating "direct painting" seem to have gotten on well together. WBY tells us in *Autobiographies* that he was not "of Stevenson's party," but that the critic would sit "at our house . . . surrounded by my brother and sisters and a little group of my father's friends."[46] It is unlikely that JBY would not have read what proved to be the critic's most important contribution to the art literature of the period. In 1899 Stevenson published a book on Velázquez (1599-1660) in which he calls the old master "the great Spanish Impressionist."[47] As a student of Carolus-Duran, Stevenson had developed a preference for tone over line, for capturing the momentary impression of the subject over mere exactitude. Indebted as he was to his teacher, Stevenson saw the technique as stemming from Velázquez. To Stevenson impressionism had a long history in European art, his notion of the phenomenon being "that images should be built up by planes alone, rather than by secondary drawing, and that surfaces remain distinct and not brushed into one another."[48] A look at some of JBY's drawings of the 1890s (nos. 17, 19, and 22) will show how the artist sought to achieve similar effects. It is worth reading Stevenson's reminiscences, from his days with Duran, of how a painting was put together:

> No preparation in colour or monochrome was allowed, but the main planes of the face must be laid directly on the prepared canvas with a broad brush. These few surfaces— three or four in the forehead, as many in the nose, and so forth—must be studied in shape and place, and particularly in the relative value of light that their various inclinations produce. They were painted quite broadly in even tones of flesh tint, and stood side by side like pieces of a mosaic, without fusion of their adjacent edges. No brushing of the edge of the hair into the face was permitted, no conventional bounding of eyes and features with lines that might deceive the student by their expression into the belief that false structure was truthful. In the next stage you were bound to proceed in the same manner by laying planes upon the junctions of the larger ones or by breaking the larger planes into smaller subordinate surfaces. You were never allowed to brush one surface into another, you must make a tone for each step of a gradation. Thus, you might never attempt to realize a tone or a passage by some hazardous uncontrollable process.
>
> M. Carolus-Duran believed that if you do not approach tone by direct painting you will never know what you can do, and will never discover whether you really feel any given relations, or the values of any contrasting surfaces.[49]

Yeats's work of the nineties (including the Defoe sketches, Fig. 8) illustrates this direct method of application. In a work such as **Jenny Mitchell** (no. 20) one notices the subtle gradation of tone that is composed of various planes of light. In his ambition to retain the quality of the initial sketch JBY was naturally sympathetic to Stevenson's ideas, but the end result is closer to a form of naturalism than impressionism. In his study of English Impressionists and post-Impressionists, Simon Watney has pointed out that the use of the term "Impressionism" in the London of the 1890s was applied not only to the new subject matter of an artist like Walter Sickert (1860-1941) but also to a general sense of cultural radicalism, like the Bohemianism which in London had been identified with the career of Whistler. "Impressionism" was also used as a general term to describe the dark tonality and attention to brushwork advocated by Stevenson.[50] Yeats best reflected the last of these three definitions. He incorporated the tonal naturalism of the post-Carolus-Duran school but also strove to capture the moment, as he had seen it observed in Whistler's graphic works. The artist's choice of subject matter during this period, as in no. 22, the image of a woman who has fallen asleep while reading a book, shows Yeats's acquiescence to the then prevalent Cult of Beauty. It would have been difficult for JBY to have avoided it, for as a resident of the culturally chic Bedford Park Yeats lived within a community of artists and writers (his own sons WBY and Jack Yeats not the least among them) and miscellaneous followers of Aestheticism.[51]

In *Velázquez* Stevenson wrote of artists who "have not been taught from the beginning in an impressionist school" and of how they "must remember difficulties which beset them when they were working from nature and will recall how they only slowly began to appreciate the meaning and the necessity of working from a single impression. How often it seemed to them impossible to finish a picture. The more closely they applied themselves to study and complete a part, the more it seemed to change to their eyes, and to invalidate their previous observations."[52] Instead the artist should aim for the "impression of the whole" and thus achieve a more satisfying unity. It may be possible to read the above remarks as a commentary on JBY's lifelong incapacity to finish a work satisfactorily. As an art critic, Stevenson almost certainly saw work by JBY, and in the light of his advice the artist may have attempted to develop what he considered an impressionist element in his work.

An acceptance of Stevenson's version of impressionism and a strong admiration for Whistler's style and subject matter are the most important stylistic and intellectual components of Yeats's art at the close of the nineteeth century. The debt to Whistler is particularly clear in a drawing such as **Lily Yeats Reclining** (no. 19) where the Irish artist pays homage to the American's superb prints of women, particularly those seated or recumbent. The well-known **Weary** (Fig. 10), a drypoint of 1863, is one of hundreds of images of somewhat indolent women that Whistler produced from the 1860s until the turn of the century. **Weary** is on the one hand a portrait of Joanna Heffernan, "the beautiful Irish girl," but on the other, it is a most emphatically male view of conscious female languor. It is certainly more than mere coincidence that Yeats's drawings of solitary women, also reclining, seated, sleeping, or reading (nos. 16, 19, 21, 22, and 23), should have appeared in the

Fig. 10. James McNeill Whistler, *Weary*, 1863, drypoint; The British Museum, London. 7⅞ x 5⅛ inches. 19.5 x 13 cms.

Fig. 11. James McNeill Whistler, *La Belle Dame Endormie*, 1894, lithograph; The British Museum, London. 7⅞ x 6⅛ inches. 20 x 15.25 cms.

same decade as Whistler's exquisitely sensitive final lithographs that draw this most consistent of Whistlerian motifs to a conclusion (e.g., **La Belle Dame Endormie**, Fig. 11).[53] Both Whistler's and JBY's women recall the Pre-Raphaelite female and, in particular, Rossetti's innumerable drawings of Elizabeth Siddall. Recent commentary on the representation of Siddall has focused on her extremely passive role and on Rossetti's deliberate creation of a feminine "look," which he as creator could then proceed to "own."[54] Whistler's women, although avoiding the excessive wistfulness of the Pre-Raphaelite, continue to embody the Victorian concept of feminine lassitude and silence. Such passivity is maintained by JBY, especially in the images of his wife (no. 10), his daughter (no. 19), and his friends (no. 22). From what we know of the Yeats women in the 1890s, their lives were greatly confined by JBY's penury, a significant consequence of which was the unmarried status of the sisters Lily and Lollie. Although doubtlessly cognizant of the difficulties in his daughters' lives, JBY in his drawings only increases the awareness of female inactivity. A sketch such as **Lily Yeats Reclining** (no. 19) thus becomes not just an intimate reflection of the artist's mood, or the chance capturing of a moment in time, but also the encapsulation of a male view of woman as having a singular visual appearance, that is, passive.

Discussion of Yeats's drawings of his daughters leads to some observations on his depiction of the male members of his family. The sketches of William (nos. 13 and 17) that date from the last decade of the century are of a dreamy poet whose intellectual vigor is consistently conveyed. In the early years of the new century Yeats was to produce many portraits of the male world of writers, artists, and bohemians. The active intellectuality of WBY (no. 17), as compared with the introverted passivity of Lily Yeats (no. 19), is achieved through the spectator's proximity to the poet, whose firmly placed arms strengthen the solidity of his presence. A sharp shadow falls across Lily's face, while her brother is lit from the spectator's direction. Lily is locked into a private world, her sideward gaze and her folded arms preventing us from entering the picture.

Yeats's return to Dublin in 1901 led to a slow yet distinguishable rise in the appreciation of his art. The retrospective exhibition of his work that heralded the return fostered further commissions and an increased optimism for the aging artist. The exhibition was organized by Sarah Purser, an Irish portraitist, who prevailed upon the reclusive landscape artist Nathaniel Hone (1831-1917) to exhibit alongside JBY.[55] The two-man exhibition was a great success, and the critic for *The Irish Times* commented most favorably on JBY's work:

Mr. Yeats is diametrically opposed to those artists who seem to care less for the spirit of man than the body—less for the body than the clothes. . . . Mr. Yeats has no affinities with this school. He suggests much rather, though at a distance, Mr. Watts. There is the same preoccupation with character, the same indifference to the special advantages of his medium—the same difficult and laboured execution, so unlike the dash and showiness of Mr. Sargent's followers.[56]

In his preoccupation with portraying conviction and character, Yeats saw his style as the opposite of the academic, of what he himself called the art of the virtuoso. The opposition led him to criticize sharply the work of the then rising stars of British portraiture, the academic school represented by William Orpen and the virtuosi by Augustus John. Repeated discussion of Orpen's work appears in JBY's letters from 1904 until his departure for New York in 1907.[57] His concern with Orpen was prompted by Hugh Lane's 1904 commission to both artists (JBY then being in his mid-sixties and Orpen only in his mid-twenties) to paint some twenty portraits of famous Irish men and women.[58]

As stated earlier, Yeats believed that his style and approach were "modern and impressionist." The artist made the claim when comparing his work with that of Orpen, which he saw as "learned—like an old master." The Lane commission as it is described in Yeats's letters takes on the appearance of a sparring match between the two painters. Yeats referred to it as a "competition"[59] and greatly comforted himself in knowing that he was a "born portrait painter" while Orpen was merely derivative. Orpen lacked subtlety in modelling and did not understand the older artist's belief in the necessity to capture the "essentials, to concentrate on character."[60] In a letter to WBY of about 1906, JBY wrote that Orpen "cannot model the delicate gradations, that make for finer expression—In these finer expressions I excel, and lately I have been trying to acquire knowledge of how to give the broader and bolder effects. Everyone who comes in is struck by the improvement in my work."[61] The full consequences of his improvements are to be found in the numerous drawings (see no. 38) that accompanied his work on an oil self-portrait commissioned in New York by John Quinn in 1911. But before turning to this later period in JBY's career we must look at the other victims of JBY's epistolary wrath, the virtuosi painters, particularly the young Augustus John (1879-1961). In 1911, writing to his American friend John Quinn, who owned some John works, JBY distinguished between "the artist who is all virtuoso" and "the artist of conviction," the latter having, he claims, "the finer execution, the finer style." "The artist of conviction is more anxious about his subject than about his painting—his painting is for the sake of his subject—he loses himself in his subject and thus attains to the best execution. The virtuoso is only interested in his painting, in his technique. We sometimes say of a man that he has become 'mannered,' that means that he has become a virtuoso."[62] To Yeats, John's portraits exhibited displaced anxiety for the painting of a picture rather than for its subject. In the letter quoted above Yeats goes on to tell Quinn that while Charles Shannon, a British artist also represented in Quinn's collection, could "paint a head better than John . . . the other

paints the coat better—both are men of conviction—only the one thinks nobly of his fellow mortals and the other regards the coat and the man who wear it as of equal interest." It was JBY's ambition, when faced with the rival portraiture of Orpen or John, to boast of how much more sensitive a portraitist he himself was and how he could "beat them all."

JBY's experimentations with what he called "broader and bolder" effects were to come to fruition after his departure for New York in late 1907. A greater looseness and a greater speed in the application of shading are evident in a drawing such as **Table at Petitpas** (no. 29), or in single portraits such as those of Mary Shaw and Jeanne Robert Foster (nos. 31 and 37). The brisk parallel pencil lines and the tendency for strokes to terminate in elaborate squiggles are noticeable features of his later work, though his attention to the faces of his sitters is still as concentrated as before. The delicate, almost minimalist, cross-hatching of the face of **Sara Allgood** (no. 35, 1911), similar to the earlier sketch of Lady Gregory (no. 28, 1907), shows the abiding interest in what the artist referred to as "the concrete life" as opposed to "the things of the imagination," from which, as he told WBY in a letter from New York, he had turned away in the 1870s when he did not accept Rossetti's invitation to visit after Rossetti had admired **Pippa Passes.**[63]

His interest in the "concrete life," his striving for an honesty in the portrayal of character, dominates JBY's notion of portraiture. From his early days as a student at the Heatherley's Art School, where he had witnessed the death throes of Pre-Raphaelitism, through the impact of Whistlerian naturalism and the intellectual acuity of G. F. Watts, to the now completely different world of early twentieth-century New York, Yeats strove to express an intensity and a presence in his sitters that would reflect his own supremely cerebral approach to human relations.

The artist's delight in conversation, discussion, and intellectual discovery is complemented in his pencil sketches by what can be termed his concern for the capturing of private concentration. Drawings from his American period such as the **Allgood** (no. 35), **Dolly Sloan** (no. 33), and his own **Self-Portrait** (no. 38) most sensitively convey the artist's lifelong preoccupation with character and truth to nature and his perceptive questioning of the human condition. Above all else, JBY's American years were dominated by the saga of the self-portrait. This was a commissioned oil that began life in 1911 but remained unfinished at the artist's death in 1922.[64] While engaged on this painting, in preparation for which he produced an unending number of pencil sketches of his tall thin frame, the artist became friendly with the young painters John Sloan, Robert Henri, and William Glackens, as well as many writers and critics. These would come to dine at Yeats's boardinghouse in New York City and savor the originality of the old man's mind. Such an occasion is celebrated in Sloan's painting, **Yeats at Petitpas** (Fig. 12).

Fig. 12. John Sloan, *Yeats at Petitpas*, 1910, oil on canvas; The Corcoran Gallery of Art, Washington, D.C. 26⅜ x 32¼ inches. Seated at the table left to right the group reads: Van Wyck Brooks, JBY, Alan Seeger, Dolly Sloan, Celestine Petitpas (standing), Robert W. Sneddon, Eulabee Dix, John Sloan, Frederick A. King (at foot of table), Mrs. Charles Johnston (at nearside of table).

Yeats's friendship with New York artists, and with Sloan (1871-1951) in particular, prompts one to ask whether the younger men had any marked influence on his late work. In the early years of the **Self-Portrait** Yeats mentions that by "working under the critical eyes of Sloan at his studio I learned a lot."[65] What Yeats learned from Sloan he described in an article for *Harper's Weekly* of November 1913, in which he said Sloan was "an impressionist, that is, an imaginative painter, and paints by the inner life, his subject directing him." JBY admired "Sloan's severity." "One has to live many days with one of his pictures to find its sweetness, its poetic charm." The imaginative power and "inner life" of Sloan's art led Yeats to speak of "the richly coloured darkness" of a painting like Sloan's **McSorley's Back Room** (1912; Hood Museum of Art, Dartmouth University, Hanover, New Hampshire). Yeats wrote that one could "never be tired of peering in that gloom." Some of Yeats's sketches for his **Self-Portrait** (no. 38) are inscribed "Myself seen through a glass darkly," the face being drawn with a greater attention to shadow than is usual in his work. It is possible that this was done on the advice of Sloan, who received sympathetic criticism from Yeats and may have attempted to return the same in kind. Chiaroscuro, Yeats said when writing of Sloan's work, "is to make a picture of infinity." JBY could have been referring to himself, especially as the creator of the numerous self-portrait sketches, when characterizing Sloan as "the artist and poet, solitary, self-immersed in his own thoughts," with "no desire to impress other people," but with "the kind of spontaneity which makes his pictures refreshing to the eye wearied with conventional art." Yeats and Sloan could share equally an artistic "message . . . that human nature has a perennial charm."[66]

JBY's New York exile was a lonely experience. He kept up an extraordinarily energetic correspondence with his sons Willie and Jack and his daughter Lily, as well as with numerous old Dublin friends. Yet, although cut off from his past, he stubbornly refused to return home. He loved the variety and excitement of New York and America and the friends he made there. And in a letter of 1915 to Jack B. Yeats, JBY, now in his mid-seventies, observed that "after the war there will be a need for portraits, and . . . I will come in handy."[67]

In his letters home and especially in those to WBY, the artist seems to have found a whole new world of expression. Similarly, the **Self-Portrait** came to act as a kind of obsessive voyage of self-discovery. Over the years of gestation (to use the artist's own word) the **Self-Portrait** became a comfort and a companion, situated as the canvas was in Yeats's small, gloomy boardinghouse room. The innumerable pencil sketches of himself which he drew in preparation for the oil were the result of his incapacity to concentrate on the canvas for any length of time. Although the painting filled his life,[68] and did so for eleven years, he would not work on it for any great length of time, but "only when the spirit moves me,"[69] or, as he wrote to Jack, "Every day I study it and occasionally I paint."[70] JBY drew himself before a mirror, pencil in hand, his dark sharp eyes staring straight ahead. The end result was the more than three-quarter-length unfinished oil, which went through years of being scrubbed out and repainted, and was the cause of occasional bursts of anger from both Sloan and Quinn, for Yeats would never leave the thing alone. The image is that of an old man with a half-smile, surrounded by pots and brushes, behind him a shabby bookcase piled high with his greatly loved books. JBY was a tall man; in his final oil he has grown lean and angular, but his face and head—"his beautiful mischievous head," as WBY described it in a late poem—are full of the curiosity and liveliness that make his letters such delightful reading, add substance to his oils, and, more particularly, in the context of this exhibition, make his drawings worthy of extensive study.

Notes to Essay

1 Denis Donoghue, "John Butler Yeats," *Abroad in America: Visitors to the New Nation, 1776-1914* (ed. Marc Pachter and Frances Wein), National Portrait Gallery, Washington, D.C. (1976), p. 265.

2 JBY to Ruth Hart, 26 August 1908. Hone, Joseph, ed., *J.B. Yeats: Letters to His Son W.B. Yeats and Others* (New York: E.P. Dutton, 1946), p. 111. JBY added: "...and sometimes the chimera of art."

3 Donoghue, p. 265.

4 *Ibid.*

5 *A Loan Collection of Pictures by Nathaniel Hone RHA and John Butler Yeats RHA, October-November, 1901, at 6 St Stephen's Green, Dublin.* JBY exhibited 43 works. The catalogue carried an "Appreciation" by his friend Frederick York Powell. In 1904 he took part in a large exhibition of Irish art originated by Hugh Lane at the Guildhall in London, where he showed four works; see Murphy, William M. *Prodigal Father: The Life of John Butler Yeats (1839-1922)* (Ithaca and London: Cornell University Press, 1978), p. 241.

6 E.J.G., "Loan Exhibition of Paintings by Mr. Hone RHA and Mr. Yeats RHA," *The Irish Times*, 21 October 1901.

7 Thomas Bodkin, "John Butler Yeats RHA," *The Dublin Magazine*, I, 6 (January 1924), p. 483.

8 *W.B. Yeats: A Centenary Exhibition*, (National Gallery of Ireland, Dublin March-April, 1965); this was the most important exhibition of the centenary. JBY was again rather inadequately discussed in the exhibition catalogue, *Jack B. Yeats and His Family*, (Sligo County Library and Museum, Sligo 1971), pp. 9, 30-36.

9 James White, *John Butler Yeats and the Irish Renaissance* (Dublin: Dolmen, 1972).

10 Most of the biographical information on JBY contained in this essay is taken from Murphy, *Prodigal Father*.

11 For recent surveys of 19th Century Irish art, see Cyril Barrett, *Irish Art in the 19th Century*, (exhibition catalogue, Crawford Municipal School of Art, Cork 1971); and Anne Crookshank and the Knight of Glin, *Painters of Ireland, c. 1660-1920* (London: Barrie and Jenkins, 1978).

12 Murphy, p. 53.

13 P. 61.

14 P. 67.

15 "God with Eyes Turned Inward Upon His Own Glory" is reproduced in Thomas Wright, *The Life of John Payne* (London: Unwin, 1919), facing p. 30. O'Shaughnessy's book is entitled *Epic of Women and Other Poems* (London: John Camden Hotten, 1870).

16 Unpublished letter from JBY to Edward Dowden, 18 January 1869 (Trinity College, Dublin); information supplied by William M. Murphy.

17 Murphy, pp. 68f.

18 *Loan Museum of Art Treasures* (Dublin Industrial Exhibition, Dublin, 1873), Fine Art Section, no. 620. A century later the drawing was included in the exhibition, *Irish Art in the Nineteenth Century*, (Crawford Municipal School of Art, Cork 1971), no. 135, p. 77, plate 24.

19 See the exhibition catalogue, *Frederick Sandys*, by Betty Elzea, (Brighton Museum and Art Gallery 1974).

20 Murphy, p. 57

21 JBY to Edward Dowden 18 January 1869 (TCD). See note 17.

22 Murphy, p. 83.

23 P. 103.

24 Bruce Laughton, *The Slade, 1871-1971*, (exhibition catalogue, Royal Academy, London, 1971) p. 5; see also Christopher Wood, *Olympian Dreamers* (London: Constable, 1983), chapter 4.

25 *From Realism to Symbolism: Whistler and His World*, (Wildenstein, New York and the Philadelphia Museum of Art, 1971), pp. 11f.

26 Unpublished letter from JBY to Susan Pollexfen Yeats, 28 October 1872. Collection: Michael B. Yeats; information supplied by William M. Murphy.

27 See Virginia Surtees, *The Paintings and Drawings of Dante Gabriel Rossetti (1828-1882). A Catalogue Raisonné*, 2 vols. (Oxford: Clarendon Press, 1971); pp. 25 f. in vol. 2; see plates 424-429, vol. 2.

28 Douglas Cooper, *The Courtauld Collection: A Catalogue and Introduction* (London: University of London, Courtauld Institute of Art, 1954), pp. 19-24.

29 See *Fantin-Latour*, (exhibition catalogue, National Gallery of Canada, Ottawa 1983).

30 Katherine A. Lochnan, *The Etchings of James McNeill Whistler*, (New Haven and London: Yale University Press, 1984), p. 128.

31 Unpublished letter from JBY to Edward Dowden, 25 April 1869 (Trinity College, Dublin); information and transcription supplied by William M. Murphy.

32 Thomas Bodkin, *op. cit.*

33 J.B. Yeats, *Essays Irish and American* (Dublin: Talbot Press, 1918), "Watts and the Method of Art," pp. 75-95, especially p. 78. On the exhibition see Murphy, p. 295. The lecture was first published in the Dublin journal, *The Shanachie*, March 1907 (Spring), pp. 113-126.

34 *Essays Irish and American*, p. 78. For recent discussion on Watts see Allen Stalley's essay in the exhibition catalogue *Victorian High Renaissance* (Minneapolis: Minneapolis Institute of Arts, 1978), pp. 54f.; also Christopher Wood, *op. cit.*, chapter 2.

35 *Essays Irish and American*, pp 79-80. See also the quotation on pp. 13-14, in Murphy's essay in this volume.

36 *Ibid.*

37 The poem appears in *Leisure Hour*, vol. 36 (1887), p. 636, with illustration facing.

38 *Great Victorian Pictures, Their Paths to Fame* (London: Arts Council of Great Britain, Royal Academy, London, 1978), no. 63, p. 88.

39 JBY supplied 17 illustrations to *The Dreams of Dania*. The story was published in book form the following year with four illustrations by JBY; see Murphy, p. 199.

40 George A. Aitken, ed., *Romances and Narratives by Daniel Defoe* (London: Dent, 1895).

41 Lily Yeats has written that she was the model for nearly every character in the Defoe commission, except for that of Man Friday; see Murphy, p. 579, n. 42.

42 James Thorpe, *English Illustration: The Nineties* (London: Hacker Art Books, 1975), p. 10.

43 Michael Quick, "Abbey as Illustrator," *Edwin Austin Abbey, 1852-1911*, (exhibition catalogue, New Haven: Yale University Art Gallery, 1973), p. 29.

44 JBY to WBY, Hone, p. 57.

45 Simon Watney, *English Post-Impressionism* (London: Trefoil Books, 1980), chapter 2.

46 *Autobiographies*, "Four Years: 1887-1891," pp. 132-33.

47 *Velázquez* (London: 1899), p. 125. In 1962 the book was reissued, the text being revised and annotated by Theodore Crombie and supplemented by a useful biographical study of Stevenson by Denys Sutton. An earlier version of the book was in fact first published in 1895 as *The Art of Velazquez*, but was much revised for the 1899 publication. Stevenson's importance has been noted by, among others, Bruce Laughton, *Philip Wilson Steer, 1860-1942* (Oxford: Clarendon Press, 1971), pp. 65-67; Simon Watney, *op. cit.*, p. 14; and Michael Jacobs, *The Good and Simple Life: Artists Colonies in Europe and America* (Oxford: Phaidon, 1985), pp. 27-32.

48 Watney, chapter 2.

49 *Velázquez*, pp. 107-08.

50 Watney, pp. 12-16.

51 For a discussion of Bedford Park and its residents, see Mark Glazebrook, *Artists and Architecture of Bedford Park, 1875-1900* (London: Shenval

Press, 1967); Ian Fletcher, "Bedford Park: Esthete's Elysium?," *Romantic Mythologies* (New York: Barnes and Noble, 1967); and Murphy, *Prodigal Father*, pp. 117ff. and p. 580.

52 *Velázquez*, pp. 122-23.

53 For a recent discussion of this motif see David Park Curry, *James McNeill Whistler, at the Freer Gallery of Art, Smithsonian Institution* (Washington, D.C.: 1984), pp. 46-47.

54 Giselda Pollock and Deborah Cherry, "Woman as Sign in Pre-Raphaelite Literature: A Study of the Representation of Elizabeth Siddall," *Art History*, vol. 7, no. 2 (June 1984), pp. 206-277.

55 See n. 8.

56 E.J.G., *The Irish Times*, 21 October 1901.

57 Murphy, *passim*, and Hone, *passim.*

58 Murphy, p. 271, and Bruce Arnold, *Orpen* (J. Cape, 1981). pp. 139-41.

59 JBY to WBY, Hone, p. 75.

60 E.J.G., *The Irish Times*, 21 October 1901.

61 Hone, p. 90.

62 Unpublished letter from JBY to Quinn, 14 March 1911; transcription by William M. Murphy, who supplied this information. The letter is now part of the Foster-Murphy Collection at the New York Public Library.

63 Unpublished letter from JBY to WBY, 25 June 1921; transcription by William M. Murphy, who supplied this information; see Murphy, p. 76. Collection of Michael B. Yeats.

64 Murphy, pp. 384f.

65 Unpublished letter from JBY to Jack Yeats, 19 May 1914; information supplied by William M. Murphy. Collection of Anne B. Yeats.

66 "The Work of John Sloan," *Harper's Weekly*, 22 November 1913, p. 21.

67 Unpublished letter from JBY to Jack Yeats, 22 July 1915; transcription by William M. Murphy who supplied this information. Collection of Anne B. Yeats.

68 Murphy, p. 524.

69 P. 430.

70 P. 498.

Abbreviations to Catalogue:

l.	left
r.	right
l.l.	lower left
l.r.	lower right
l.c.	lower center
cat. no.	catalogue number
cms.	centimeters
c.r.	center right
illus.	illustration
Inscr.	Inscription
Prov.	Provenance
Ref.	References
R.H.A.	Royal Hibernian Academy (Academician)
Exh.	Exhibition
JBY	John Butler Yeats
WBY	William Butler Yeats

Dublin, 1901.	*A Loan Collection of Pictures by Nathaniel Hone RHA and John Butler Yeats RHA,* October-November, 1901, at 6 St Stephen's Green, Dublin.
Hone.	Joseph Hone, ed., *J. B. Yeats: Letters to His Son W. B. Yeats and Others, 1869-1922* (New York: Dutton, 1946).
Murphy.	William M. Murphy, *Prodigal Father: The Life of John Butler Yeats (1839-1922)* (Ithaca and London: Cornell University Press, 1978).
N.G.I., 1972.	*John Butler Yeats and the Irish Renaissance*, with pictures from the collection of Michael Butler Yeats and the National Gallery of Ireland (1972); exhibition catalogue by James White (Dublin: Dolmen, 1972).

Catalogue

Fintan Cullen

1. **Enniscrone, Co. Sligo.** Summer 1866.

17.5 x 27.2 cms. 6¾ x 10½ inches.

Pen and brown ink on paper.

Inscr. (in Lily Yeats's hand): "Enniscrone, Co. Sligo."

Ref.: Wm. Murphy, *The Yeats Family and the Pollexfens of Sligo* (Dublin: Dolmen, 1971), p. 61; Murphy, illus., p. 50.

Exh.: N.G.I., 1972 (8).

The artist's earliest illustrative works were wood-block drawings that he submitted to such journals as *Fun*, and it is possible that this drawing of Enniscrone is the kind that JBY sent to London for consideration for graphic reproduction. The quality of the finely hatched pen lines and the clarity of composition suggest the cartoon manner. Less than a year later JBY had settled in London as an artist. He also spent later summers in Sligo. The artist wrote to his friend Edward Dowden in 1868: "During my stay in Ireland I shall be very busy, sketching everything which I can make useful in wood drawing. I am working very hard, 8 and 9 and 10 hours a day. I think you will recognize a great advance in my drawing. . . . I want to study and become a fully accomplished artist, and not a mere sketcher and wood draughtsman."[1]

Collection of Michael Butler Yeats.

2. **Portrait of a Girl.** c. 1866-68.

21 x 14.2 cms. 8⅛ x 5⅜ inches.

Pen and black ink on paper.

Exh.: N.G.I., 1972 (12).

Like the sketch of Enniscrone (no. 1) this drawing was possibly made for wood-block printing, though its graphic representation has not come to light. As a student artist in London in the 1860s driven by necessity to supplement his income by producing wood drawings, JBY probably looked at the illustrative work of his contemporaries. The rather heavy lines of this drawing and the emphatic hatching remind one of the work of Charles Keene (1823-91), whose drawings appeared in *Punch*. JBY's drawing is also reminiscent of the rounded forms of the Pre-Raphaelite school, a fact confirmed by a comment in a letter of August 1868 to his friend Edwin Ellis, where JBY mentioned that he had "made within the last week some careful copies of [John Everett] Millais' wood drawings, with great advantage to myself, I think."[2]

Collection of Michael Butler Yeats.

3. **Corner of the Sitting Room in Fitzroy Road.** c. 1870-72.

18 x 24 cms. 6⅞ x 9¼ inches.

Watercolor with body color and gum with Chinese White on paper.

Inscr. l.r. (in Lily Yeats's hand): "Corner of the Sitting Room in Fitzroy Road."

Verso: pencil drawing of group launching a boat, with miscellaneous figure drawings.

From July 1867 to July 1873, JBY and his family lived at 23 Fitzroy Road near Regent's Park, London, the house serving as both home and studio. As a student at Heatherley's the young artist was initially attracted to the Pre-Raphaelite school, then some twenty years old. The table and objects in this drawing are executed in a finely detailed manner, the colors are rich, and the light conveys a heightened sensitivity to texture. All is in keeping with the exactitude sought by Dante Gabriel Rossetti and John Everett Millais and made into a dominant aesthetic by John Ruskin. Yet, despite the evidence of this drawing, Yeats was too much of an individualist to allow a devotion to verisimilitude to obscure his own pursuit of truth. "Only poor fellows," Yeats wrote to his friend Edwin Ellis, "who want to sell their pictures or vain ones who want to show off their skill or conscientious ones who have weak artistic individuality . . . and who are the dupes of some such irrelevancy as that 'nothing can surpass nature' will care about verisimilitude . . . . In itself it is a thing to be despised by the true artist."[3] Although it is difficult to date accurately the drawings of this period, it is clear that within a short time after the above study was drawn Yeats's art was beginning to show a striking rejection of the Ruskinian ideal.

Collection of Michael Butler Yeats.

Corner of the sitting room in Fitzroy Road

4. **Nelly Whelan.** c. 1870.

   21.5 x 13.1 cms. 8¼ x 5 inches.

   Pencil on paper.

   Inscr. l.r. (in Lily Yeats's hand): "Nelly Whelan."

   Verso: pencil sketch of a standing boy in a sailor outfit.

   Nelly Whelan was possibly the model for the drawing **Pippa Passes** (Fig. 3, 1869-72) commissioned by Yeats's friend John Todhunter. Greatly impressed by it when he viewed it over the summer of 1870, Edward Dowden asked Yeats to draw him a "study for Pippa from Nelly."[4] Although Dowden's drawing has not come to light, the exhibited sketch has similarities to the **Pippa** in its feeling for rounded forms, particularly those of the head and shoulders, and a clear, softly modelled face with tight hatching lines of pencil. In a broader context, the passivity and silence of the image together with the lowered head and compact form recall Rossetti drawings of Elizabeth Siddall and Fanny Cornforth of a decade or so earlier.[5]

   Collection of Michael Butler Yeats.

5. **Aunt Gracie Yeats.** c. 1870-73.

17.5 x 12.8 cms. 6¾ x 4⅞ inches.

Pencil on paper.

Inscr. (in Lily Yeats's hand): "Aunt Gracie Yeats."

Although still displaying the curvilinear grace of the Rossettian forms that had inspired such finished works as **Pippa Passes** (Fig. 3), this drawing indicates a growing new influence in Yeats's development. By 1873 the artist had undergone a year's tuition under Edward Poynter (1836-1919) at the Slade School of Art. Poynter seems to have encouraged Yeats to develop a greater proximity to his sitters; in this sketch the head is held high and we see how the artist has moved beyond the Pre-Raphaelite fashion of depicting women as limpid beings with heavily lidded eyes. There is a new subtlety in his use of pencil, and the face is delicately modelled with a sensitive use of light, qualities found also in the splendid sweep of the arm. The artist's sister, Gracie (1846-1935), is here shown in what is possibly a study for an untraced oil painting completed in the spring of 1873.[6]

Collection of Michael Butler Yeats.

Aunt pacil Yeats

6. **William Butler Yeats as a Boy.** c. 1872-74.

17.7 x 25.4 cms. 6¾ x 9¾ inches.

Pencil on paper.

Inscr. l.r. (in ink in Lily Yeats's hand): "W. B. Yeats."

Ref.: Wm. Murphy, *The Yeats Family and the Pollexfens of Sligo* (Dublin: Dolmen, 1971), no. 5, p. 63; *Times Literary Supplement*, 17 March 1972, p. 292; Murphy, illus. p. 100.

Exh.: N.G.I., 1972 (13).

Like no. 5, this sketch is a manifestation of the growing dissatisfaction that Yeats felt in the early 1870s with the Pre-Raphaelite style. The emphatically rounded forms of his earlier works have been curtailed in favor of a more angular and less patterned presentation. As WBY was born in 1865, he was about nine when this sketch was made. The boy has been placed a foot or so away from a wall, his dark shadow creating depth and emphasizing the solidity of the figure. An acquaintance with contemporary French painters, in particular Fantin-Latour, and with Whistler is now beginning to appear in the artist's work. The naturalism of the new French school, with its subject matter of ordinary domestic moments, is here rendered in a controlled and highly sensitive manner. Although it is difficult to look at this drawing without seeing it merely as a sketch of the brooding young William Butler Yeats, it is first and foremost part of a highly personal series of studies by a father of his children.

Collection of Michael Butler Yeats.

7. **Jack B. Yeats as a Boy.** 1875.

13.3 x 6.5 cms. 5¼ x 3⅛ inches.

Pencil on paper, backed.

Inscr. l.l. (in artist's hand): "Nov. 18th/1875."

Verso: in pencil: "Mrs. Yeats 14 Edith Villas, Fulham."[7]

Ref.: Murphy, illus., p. 108.

Jack Yeats (1871-1957) was about four years old when the drawing was done. He, too, became an artist, but, unlike his father, enjoyed considerable fame as one of the leading Irish painters of the first half of the twentieth century. In contrast to the sketch of his brother (no. 6), Jack is drawn in a far less experimental style, the lines being soft and rounded as in no. 4, a drawing of some four or five years earlier. Although the piece does not indicate the struggle that JBY was having between the legacy of the English school and the attractions of the new ideas coming from France, it does convey the artist's control over his pencil. He has now become adept at the quick sketch, and a personal style is beginning to emerge, here shown by the delicate hatching of the face, the alternation between heavily and lightly applied pencil, and the penchant for odd angles and compositions.

Collection of Anne Butler Yeats.

8. **Lollie Yeats with a Ball.** 1877.

18 x 13.3 cms. 6⅞ x 5¼inches.

Pencil and grey wash on paper pasted onto another sheet of paper.

Inscr. l.r. (in artist's hand): "June 3rd 1877."

Ref.: Wm. Murphy, *The Yeats Family and the Pollexfens of Sligo* (Dublin: Dolmen, 1971), p. 64.

Elizabeth Corbet Yeats (1868-1940), called "Lollie," was about nine when drawn by her father in this sketch. JBY's growing preoccupation with the face of his sitter is here expressed with an intensity that is greatly aided by the addition of some grey wash to the underlying pencil. The tonal quality thus created highlights the girl's large eyes and indicates, yet again, the artist's growing attraction for the work of Fantin-Latour, who from 1871 was exhibiting annually at the Winter Exhibition of the Dudley Gallery, London.

Collection of Michael Butler Yeats.

9. **Lily Yeats Reading.** c. 1876-77.

6.90 x 12 cms. 2⅝ x 4⅝ inches.

Pen and brown ink on paper.

Ref.: Murphy, *The Yeats Family and the Pollexfens of Sligo* (Dublin: Dolmen, 1971), p. 65.

This sketch of the artist's first daughter, Susan Mary Yeats (1866-1949), known as "Lily," was made on a black-rimmed bereavement envelope.[8] Although similar in composition and subject to the drawing of Nelly Whelan (no. 4), it displays the greater degree of naturalism that entered JBY's work as the 1870s progressed. The earlier drawing of c. 1870 is as much concerned with the curvilinear patterns as with the portrayal of character. In this tiny portrait of his daughter the artist eschews pattern for direct observation. JBY, like Whistler in his drawings (c. 1872-74) of Elinor ("Baby") Leyland, daughter of Frederick Leyland of Liverpool, used the motif of a girl or woman reading on a number of occasions; see nos. 4, 10, and 22.

Collection of Michael Butler Yeats.

10. **Susan Pollexfen Yeats.** c. 1882-84.

47.5 x 35 cms. 18½ x 13⅝ inches.

Black chalk and charcoal on paper backed on board.

Ref.: Murphy, illus., p. 128.

Susan Pollexfen (1841-1900) married JBY in 1863. This large drawing is a more fully realized example than has been evident heretofore of JBY's tendency towards a greater interest in the face than in other parts of the body. The sitter's hands and the chair on which she sits are left unfinished, while the head, turned to the left, is rendered in a soft yet precise manner. One's attention is naturally drawn to the face, in which one finds a taut intensity.[9]

In *Reveries over Childhood and Youth* (1914) WBY relates that in the early 1880s, due to his own preoccupation with the Cult of Beauty, he frequently quarrelled with his father over the naturalist tendencies in the latter's portraiture.[10] Meanwhile JBY assisted in the organization of an exhibition of Whistler's paintings in Dublin, thus bringing to the city such works as the then infamous portrait of Whistler's mother, **Arrangement in Grey and Black** (1871; Musée du Louvre, Paris).[11] Although appreciative of the American artist, WBY was not amused by a remark of his father's, "Imagine making your old mother an arrangement in grey!"[12] It is possible that the exhibited chalk drawing was done around this time, the dark shaded quality having a clearly Whistlerian tone. Although compositionally very different from Whistler's painting, Susan Yeats's silence and the sideward turn of the head could be said to have some affinities with the mood of **Arrangement in Grey and Black**.

Collection of Anne Butler Yeats.

11. **William Morris and Two Unidentified Men.**[13] c. 1885.

16.8 x 24 cms. 6½ x 9¼ inches.

Pencil on paper.

Inscr. l.r. (in ink in Lily Yeats's hand): "William Morris."

Verso: portrait in pencil of a man and a drawing of a doorway.

JBY greatly admired William Morris (1834-96), whom he drew on at least one other occasion; the drawing is now in the National Gallery of Ireland (see Murphy, illus., p. 147). One of the sketches of Morris was drawn on the spot at the Contemporary Club in Dublin, the other probably done there also. The club was founded in 1885, members having in common only that they were sympathetic to Home Rule and were all alive at the same moment.[14] JBY and WBY attended regularly, as did such political and cultural figures as Douglas Hyde, Michael Davitt, and John O'Leary (see no. 25). The members discussed social, political, and literary questions of the day, and JBY's membership gave him access to many interesting people, whose portraits he sketched.[15] By the 1880s JBY had found a mode which perfectly suited his approach to portraiture. This mode, best referred to as Whistlerian, favored quick execution and concentration on the head, the outer areas being treated with what almost approaches disdain.

Collection of Michael Butler Yeats.

William Morris

12. **Two Members of Parliament.** c. 1885.

14.9 x 23 cms. 5⅝ x 8⅞ inches.

Pencil on paper.

Inscr. l.l. (in the artist's hand): "Xavier O'Brien MP"; c.r. (in the artist's hand): "Dr Ainsworth MP."

Like the sketch of William Morris (no. 11) these quickly executed drawings were done at the Contemporary Club. James Francis Xavier O'Brien (1831-95), of the Irish Nationalist party, was a member of Parliament for Mayo South (1885-95). His colleague David Ainsworth (1842-1906) was an Englishman who favored Home Rule for Ireland and sat as a National Liberal for Cumberland West (1880-85).

Collection of Michael Butler Yeats.

Xavier O'Brien MP.

Dr. Cumming. MP.

13. **William Butler Yeats.** 1889.

10 x 17.7 cms. 3¾ x 6⅞ inches.

Black wash with white highlighting over pencil on blue paper.

Inscr. l.r. (in Lily Yeats's hand): "June 1889."

Ref.: Wm. Murphy, *The Yeats Family and the Pollexfens of Sligo* (Dublin: Dolmen, 1971), p. 68.

JBY drew and painted innumerable portraits of WBY, far more than of any of his other children. Many of these were used as frontispieces to the poet's work or were commissioned by his admirers. This sketch may have been a preparatory study for a portrait. WBY had by this time already published some verse and was described by Katherine Tynan as "in looks . . . as picturesque as one could desire—hair, beard and beautiful eyes of a southern darkness, with a face of a fine oval, and a clear dusky colour. . . . Nature has written the poet upon his face."[16]

In 1887, some two years before this drawing was made, JBY had been commissioned by the magazine *Leisure Hour* to provide an illustration to accompany his son's poem "King Goll," and had used the poet himself as the model for the mad king (Fig. 5).[17] Many years later, writing to Olivia Shakespear, WBY remembered his appearance during these years and recalled the image of King Goll and how he himself looked "very desirable [although] no woman noticed it at the time—with dreamy eyes and a great mass of black hair."[18] In the exhibited drawing JBY recaptured the "dreamy" look of the poet but changed his technique from line to wash. Such a change in the artist's illustrative work of the 1880s and 1890s can be explained by JBY's attraction, firmly established in those years, to the tonal subtleties of the modern French and Whistlerian schools as well as to the dramatic changes then occurring in the photomechanical reproduction of tone drawings. Technical experiments between 1880 and 1890 resulted in reproductions of far greater fidelity in gradations of tone in a drawing.[19]

Collection of Michael Butler Yeats.

June 1889

14. **A Haunted Chamber (?)**. 1899.

30.7 x 17.3 cms. 11⅞ x 6⅝ inches.

Black and grey wash with white highlighting on paper, backed on board.

Exh.: ? Royal Hibernian Academy, 1900; Dublin, 1901.

In a letter to WBY of 1899 JBY wrote of his having finished "two black and whites which you would like—the titles are suggestive 'Love's Farewell' and 'A Haunted Chamber.' "[20] Although difficult to prove, it is possible that the drawing exhibited here, because of its subject, is the second work mentioned in the artist's letter and the one he exhibited at the Royal Hibernian Academy in 1900. The dating of the drawing as of the late 1890s is in accord, stylistically, with other JBY works of the decade. In the frontispiece to Defoe's *A Journal of the Plague Year*[21] (Fig. 8) one notices how the artist creates rich dramatic effects by means of white gouache highlighting in quite dark wash drawings. The wash is applied in a planar style, the brush strokes placed quite visibly one beside the other. As will be seen in subsequent drawings, the artist further explored the possibilities of this technique in his portraits of the 1890s (see no. 16).

Collection of Michael Butler Yeats.

15. **Preparatory Sketches for *Music's Golden Tongue*.** c. 1893-94.

17.8 x 25 cms. 6⅞ x 9⅝ inches each page.

Pencil on paper: pages from a sketchbook.[22]

These sketches of a young woman and a man playing a concertina are studies for a full-page illustration entitled **Music's Golden Tongue** that appeared in an 1894 issue of the family magazine *Leisure Hour* (Fig. 13). The artist's daughter Lily was the model for much of JBY's illustrative work of the 1880s and 1890s. In the sketchbook in which these sketches appear, her features are continuously in evidence in roles ranging from peasant girl to elegant lady. There is a lyrical quality running through much of these illustrations, a lyricism that harks back to the great profusion of illustrated books during the 1860s. Yeats might have known of the wood-engraved illustrations of such an artist as G. J. Pinwell (1842-75), who specialized in rustic scenes bathed in a romantic melancholy,[23] but by the 1890s this kind of English lyricism had been affected by the peasant subjects of Jules Bastien-Lepage (1848-84), which were readily available for viewing in London throughout the 1880s and 1890s. Lepage's detailed finish and plein-air technique soon became immensely popular. Ironically, his academic realist style helped create the English Impressionist school of such artists as Walter Sickert and Wilson Steer.[24] Although JBY did not extend his subject matter to peasants in landscapes, this brief foray into the new French manner displays a distinct awareness of Lepage's highly sentimentalized pastoralist world where the light is even and expression is lessened in favor of the picturesque.[25]

Collection of Anne Butler Yeats.

Fig. 13. JBY, *Music's Golden Tongue*, *Leisure Hour*, vol. 43, 1894, p. 546.

63

16. **Lily Yeats (?) Seated in a Garden.** 1895-98.

25.5 x 15 cms. 9⅞ x 5¾ inches.

Black and grey wash over pencil on paper.

Verso: in pencil, seated woman with hands joined.

The face of the sitter is here created by means of a softly toned wash similar to that used in some of JBY's illustrative work (see no. 14). The planar technique used on the face, with its close application of the brush, is in marked contrast to the rest of the figure, which is only loosely conveyed. Yeats is here experimenting with what he incorrectly considered to be "impressionism." Following the art critic R. A. M. Stevenson's dictum "that images should be built up by planes alone, rather than by secondary drawing, and that surfaces remain distinct and not brushed into one another,"[26] JBY attempted by the mid-1890s to achieve a far greater feeling for spontaneity in his portraiture. The artist seems to have favored Stevenson's so-called impressionist technique because the tonal arrangement of form allowed for a far greater proximity, in this case to the face of the sitter, than would be possible if total dependence were placed on precision of drawing. Yeats was less interested in displaying painterly bravura or skill than in capturing the personality and character of his sitters. His wash and pencil drawings are a celebration of direct observation over what Stevenson and his friends would have considered the highly structured falsities of academic painting.

Collection of Michael Butler Yeats.

17. **William Butler Yeats Lounging in an Armchair**

c. 1895-97.

25.6 x 37 cms. 9⅞ x 14⅜ inches.

Pencil on paper.

Yeats increasingly made use of the black lead pencil during the period around the turn of the century and achieved a greater expressiveness through his increased control of it. In an "Appreciation" of the artist's work written for the catalogue of the 1901 exhibition in Dublin, JBY's friend, Frederick York Powell, wrote: "He has incontestably made the soft greys and dark sheen of the black lead the vehicle of some of his most intimate and successful interpretations of living nature."[27] Consolidating the ideas he gained from R. A. M. Stevenson and his own observations of modern French art, Yeats drew a great number of spontaneous and intimate drawings of his family and close friends. This fluidly handled sketch of his son shows a tendency towards including large dark areas which may have been inspired by Stevenson's praise of Velázquez and Manet.

Collection of Michael Butler Yeats.

18. **Woman Writing.** c.1894-95.

25.5 x 36 cms. 10 x 14⅜ inches.

Pencil on paper.

In a letter to WBY of May 20, 1899, JBY wrote that in recent years he had devoted his whole time to portrait painting, "believing my salvation to lie that way," and adding, "From 1890 to 1897 I never touched a paint brush, and altogether, unlike Miss Purser and others, I have never had full chances as regards painting."[28] A common feature of the drawings of this period is Yeats's tendency to convey a feeling of private concentration in his sitters. Here the subject is shown working at a table, an inkwell in the left foreground. By means of a series of quickly applied hatchings on the left side of the sheet, the artist conveys not only the weight of the body that is leaning on the table but also the mental concentration exerted by the sitter, whose head is lowered, and whose face is almost hidden by a lengthy fringe of hair. As with other drawings of this period (nos. 17 and 19) the part of the face that is revealed is composed of an intricate series of lightly applied lines, while the torso and arms are only summarily suggested.

Collection of Michael Butler Yeats.

19. **Lily Yeats Reclining.** c. 1897.

25.6 x 35.5 cms. 9⅞ x 13¾ inches.

Pencil on paper.

The loose pencilwork of the drawings of the 1890s can be seen as part of the pseudo-impressionism that appeared in London throughout the decade. The softly controlled lighting effects reveal the lingering debt to Whistler, a legacy that first appeared in the early 1870s in such drawings as **William Butler Yeats as a Boy** (no. 6) and was perfected in the following decade (see no. 10). In no. 19 JBY attempts to capture the surface tone of Whistler's prints as well as the seeming effortlessness of his lithographs. This drawing may be dated to around the year 1897; in December 1896 Lily Yeats returned from France where she had worked as a governess to an Anglo-Indian family. While abroad Lily had come down with typhoid fever and returned weak and uncured.[29] This sketch may date from the period of her convalescence.

Collection of Michael Butler Yeats.

20. **Jenny Mitchell.** c. 1899.

25 x 17.9 cms. 9⅝ x 7⅞ inches.

Pencil on paper.

Inscr. l.r. (in Lily Yeats's hand): "Jenny Mitchell."

Exh.: N.G.I., 1972 (41).

Jenny Mitchell was the sister of the Irish poet and literary critic Susan Mitchell (1866-1926), who lived with the Yeats family at Bedford Park, London, from 1897-99, as a companion to Lily and a paying guest.[30] The artist's overriding interest in the face of his sitters at the expense of other areas is here shown at its best. The face is composed of softly rubbed curved pencil lines, while the shoulders are reduced to a quickly executed series of parallel lines bracketed by a number of very freely drawn squiggles. As the 1890s progressed JBY favored a looser, directly pencilled or brushed technique over the precision of previous decades. This "impressionistic" technique was fundamentally *only* a technique and not a movement. As Simon Watney has pointed out in *English Post-Impressionism*, impressionism in the London of the 1890s "implied an attitude towards tonality and actual brushwork" and was discussed as "an approach to painting . . . a technique which might be discovered in all periods of European art."[31]

Collection of Michael Butler Yeats.

21. **"Cuckoo" York Powell.** c. 1895-99.

Pencil on paper.

25.5 x 17.9 cms. 9⅞ x 6⅞ inches.

Inscr. l.l. (in Lily Yeats's hand): "Cuckoo York Powell."

Exh.: Dublin, 1901.

Mariella York Powell was the daughter of JBY's close friend Frederick York Powell, who lived in Bedford Park near the artist. In JBY's drawings and paintings of children, great attention is often paid to the eyes (see Fig. 9). The result can be a slightly sentimental response (possibly what John Sloan later called the artist's tendency to be "a little sweet"), but the drawing is always done sympathetically. Cuckoo's face is drawn by means of a series of thinly pencilled lines placed one by the other, creating a tonal effect not unlike that used in the wash drawing of Lily Yeats (no. 16). As is so often the case with JBY's drawings of this period the rest of the sitter's body is given scant attention, though by allowing the child's chin to sink into her chest, the artist conveys the self-preoccupied world of the intense young girl.

Collection of Michael Butler Yeats.

22. **A Woman Dozing.** c. 1897-99.

25.5 x 17.9 cms. 9⅞ x 6⅞ inches.

Pencil on paper.

As discussed in the accompanying essay, Yeats did a large number of drawings of solitary women, reclining or seated and often reading or sleeping. Whistler's numerous etchings of his mistress Jo Heffernan and the lithographs of his wife and family (Figs. 10 and 11) have been cited for their similarities of subject matter, surface tonal effects, and the striving for economy of line and detail. At times JBY's application of the pencil became heavy. Worked areas of flat black pencil, such as those on the woman's dress, recall the abstract grey-blackness of Fantin-Latour, in particular of a painting done more than thirty years earlier, **Reading** (1863), in the Musée des Beaux Arts, Tournai.[32] What would have attracted Yeats to this kind of French painting was the lack of accessories to distract the viewer and Fantin's self-proclaimed "absolute fidelity to the model," who was to be painted "uncompromisingly from nature."[33]

Collection of Michael Butler Yeats.

23. **Cottie Yeats.** c. 1903-4.

25.2 x 19 cms. 9¾ x 7¼ inches.

Pencil on paper, backed.

Inscr. (in Lily Yeats's hand): "Cottie Yeats."

Ref.: Murphy, illus., p. 178.

Mary Cottenham White was the wife of Jack B. Yeats, whom she married in 1894. During the early years of the twentieth century JBY's soft, often rubbed pencil line gave way to a still looser manner of hatching and squiggles, the lines becoming heavier and more distinct than heretofore. This drawing shows a less tightly applied series of thin pencil lines in the face than appeared in the sketches of Jenny Mitchell (no. 20) or "Cuckoo" York Powell (no. 21). Similarly, the body and surrounding areas have become more open. By creating an interesting compositional play with the sitter's arms so that they frame her head, the artist creates a portrait study of concentrated informality.

Collection of Michael Butler Yeats.

Cttie Yeats

24. **Patrick Vincent O'Duffy, R.H.A.** 1905.

24.8 x 17.7 cms. 9⅝ x 6¾ inches.

Pencil on paper.

Inscr. (in the artist's hand): "June 3/1905/JB Yeats."

Ref.: *The Shanachie*, March 1907 (Spring), illus. opp. p. 49; Wm. Murphy, *The Yeats Family and the Pollexfens of Sligo* (Dublin: Dolmen, 1971), p. 69.

Exh.: N.G.I., 1972, illus. on the cover and p. 33. In both places and in *The Yeats Family and the Pollexfens of Sligo* the sketch is erroneously identified as a self-portrait of JBY.

JBY had an insatiable appetite for conversation and the exchange of ideas, and after returning to Dublin from London in 1901 he attracted the leading intellectual and artistic personalities of the city to his studio on St. Stephen's Green. Thomas Bodkin has remarked that JBY "drew everyone who interested him."[34] O'Duffy (1832-1909) was a painter and fellow member with JBY of the Royal Hibernian Academy and an admirer of Yeats's work.[35] As in many of his sketches, the brisk hatching of the background and of the torso contrast with the soft modelling of the face and the penetrating stare of the eyes.

Collection of Michael Butler Yeats.

25. **John O'Leary.** c. 1905.

17.8 x 25.7 cms. 6⅞ x 9⅞ inches.

Pencil on paper.

Inscr. (in ink in Lily Yeats's hand): "John O'Leary."

Verso: in pencil, head study of J. M. Synge.

Exh.: N.G.I., 1972 (60).

As stated in the accompanying essay, Yeats firmly believed that good portraiture "will be painted where the relation of the sitter and the painter is one of friendship."[36] John O'Leary (1830-1907) was a Fenian leader who had been imprisoned in 1865 for subversive activities and later became a close friend of both JBY and WBY. The artist drew a number of sketches and oil portraits (see Fig. 2) of O'Leary.[37] This drawing, with its strength of execution and the known depth of feeling that existed between painter and sitter, conveniently summarizes the two major visual strains that run through JBY's art. The artist's ability to convey personal interest and intellectual compatibility with his sitter had been nurtured, if not initially inspired, by the example of George Frederic Watts. The great Victorian's intellectually rigorous portraits of such patriarchal figures as Carlyle and Tennyson were seen by Yeats as a vital alternative to the sterility of the Pre-Raphaelites. Concurrent with this pursuit of character, Yeats from the 1870s onward was actively seeking a style that would clearly convey his approach to portraiture, and, as already mentioned, the search led him towards the immediacy and honesty of observation of the modern French school. The latter influence caused him to label himself, however erroneously, an "impressionist." One should be reminded that it was in a letter of 1904, written within a year or less of the execution of this drawing, that JBY had spoken of his being a modern. But it should also be pointed out that by 1905 three of Yeats's most seminal influences had recently died, Whistler in 1903 and both Watts and Fantin-Latour in 1904. JBY himself was in his mid-sixties. The naturalism that he had so wholeheartedly embraced was now no longer in the forefront of either British or French painting.

Collection of Michael Butler Yeats.

John O'Leary

26. **George Moore.** 1905.

50 x 40 cms. 18¾ x 15 inches

Pencil on paper.

Inscr. l.r. (in pencil in the artist's hand): "George Moore/by/JB Yeats/August 1st, 1905."

Prov.: Possibly John Quinn Collection.

Ref.: Murphy, illus., pp. 274, 286; Robert Becker, "Artists Look at George Moore," *Irish Arts Review*, vol. 2, no. 4 (Winter 1985), p. 65, no. 121.

The novelist, critic, and erstwhile artist, George Moore (1852-1933), was a founder with WBY of the Irish Literary Theatre. In 1905 JBY received the commission for a portrait of Moore from John Quinn, the New York Irish-American lawyer and art collector, who was then in the process of building up a collection of portraits of some of the leading Irish literary figures and already had oils by JBY of George Russell (AE), Standish O'Grady, and John O'Leary (Fig. 2).[38] As was his way, JBY would make interminable sketches of his sitter and then take an excessively long time finishing the oil portrait. Yeats was preoccupied with capturing the character of his sitter and not with displaying a learned style, but unfortunately the artist's "eagerness to get to the essentials"[39] greatly exasperated his patrons and, in Quinn's case, led to heated letters across the Atlantic.[40]

James Augustine Healy Collection of Irish Literature, Colby College, Waterville, Maine.

27. **John Eglinton Conversing.** 1905.

50 x 40 cms. 18¾ x 15 inches.

Pencil on paper.

Inscr. l.r. (in pencil in the artist's hand): "John Eglinton/ conversing/by/JB Yeats/July 1905."

Prov.: Possibly John Quinn Collection.

Ref.: Murphy, illus., p. 283.

John Eglinton was the literary pseudonym of William Kirkpatrick Magee (1868-1961), who was active in the Irish Literary Revival. In describing his own style as "modern and impressionist," JBY wished to separate himself from the excessively smooth, dramatic, and fashionable art of his contemporaries John Singer Sargent and William Orpen, whom he referred to as virtuosi, or "prose" painters.[41] Whistler by contrast was a "poet painter."[42] JBY closely identified himself with Whistler's wish to retain the quality of the initial sketch, so the emphasis here is on the modelling rather than on line work. The portraits of literary and cultural figures that JBY produced from 1904 to 1907, his most public works, were sources of great pleasure to the artist. During these years he was only too aware, as his letters demonstrate, of his great gifts as a portraitist. In a letter of 1904, after casting a highly critical eye on the work of William Orpen, JBY, writing with an assurance that only maturity and public acclaim (he had had a successful exhibition in 1901) could have supplied, claimed that "it is the delicate gradations that make for finer expressions—in these finer expressions I excel. . . . Everyone who comes in is struck by the improvement in my work."[43]

James Augustine Healy Collection of Irish Literature, Colby College, Waterville, Maine.

John Eglinton
convalescing—
Myrel—
Oct. 1915.

28. **Augusta Lady Gregory.** 1907.

34.3 x 24.8 cms. 13¼ x 9⅝ inches.

Pencil on paper.

Inscr. (in the artist's hand): "Lady Gregory/by/JB Yeats 1907."

Prov.: Purchased by John Quinn from the artist. Later in the collection of Millicent Rogers. (Sale, Parke-Bernet, New York, April 23, 1963.)

This portrait of one of the leading figures of the Irish Literary Revival was signed and dated in the year of JBY's departure from Ireland for the United States. As a close friend and supporter of WBY, Lady Gregory (1852-1932) had since 1897 frequently met JBY and on a number of occasions was drawn and painted by him.[44] In 1904, at the time of the commission by her nephew Hugh Lane for twenty portraits from JBY, Lady Gregory asked the artist to provide her with some pencil drawings of what she called "my best countrymen." These were of course the same people that JBY was painting for Lane and included, among others, WBY, Jack Yeats, J. M. Synge, and Lane himself.[45] Although of great historical interest, some of these portraits of literary figures lack the intimacy and the struggle to capture the personality that so enliven JBY's sketches of his family and close associates.[46] JBY never felt entirely comfortable in Lady Gregory's company, and his careless ways were the cause of great aggravation to the often tyrannical hostess of Coole Park, Co. Galway.[47]

Collection of Mr. and Mrs. J. Robert Maguire.

29. **Table at Petitpas; the Mesdemoiselles Petitpas.** c. 1909-10.

25.7 x 34.9 cms. 9⅞ x 13½ inches.

Pencil on paper.

In late 1909 JBY moved into the Petitpas boardinghouse at 317 West 29th Street, New York, where he lived until his death on February 3, 1922. The boardinghouse was run by three Breton sisters, two of whom appear in this sketch of a group playing cards.[48] As has already been noted, with the drawings from the turn of the century onwards (see no. 23) the artist's hand generally became looser and more fluid. The New York drawings, in addition, are distinguished by the greater concentration of heavy shadows on the faces. The card players are not individualized, a rare occurrence in JBY's work, but seem to have been sketched for reasons of compositional interest.

Collection of Michael Butler Yeats.

30. **Celestine Petitpas.** c. 1909-10.

12.7 x 17.8 cms. 4⅞ x 6⅞ inches.

Pencil on paper.

Inscr. l.r. (in the artist's hand) "Mlle. Petitpas/J.B. Yeats."

Prov.: John Sloan.

JBY was particularly fond of the youngest Petitpas sister, Celestine, whom he sketched many times. He also attempted an oil portrait of her which cannot now be traced.[49] Celestine, who must have been about nineteen years old when drawn by JBY,[50] figures as the standing waitress in John Sloan's contemporaneous painting **Yeats at Petitpas** (1910; Corcoran Gallery of Art, Washington, D.C.; Fig. 12). The Wilmington sketch captures her in a not too dissimilar expression, the head slightly to the side, her eyes lowered, half her face and her left shoulder in shadow.

Delaware Art Museum, Wilmington; Gift of Helen Farr Sloan.

31. **Mary Shaw.** c. 1909-10.

17.8 x 12.7 cms. 6⅞ x 4⅞ inches.

Pencil on paper.

Inscr. l.l. (in the artist's hand): "Mary Shaw"; signed l.c.: "JB Yeats."

Verso: very free sketch of women, animated, in conversation.

Prov.: John Sloan.

On arriving in New York JBY stayed for some time at the Grand Union Hotel which was owned by a Samuel Shaw and his brother-in-law Simeon Ford.[51] The sitter of the sketch may have been Shaw's wife or daughter. During his first two years in the city JBY attracted a number of society ladies from whom he received commissions and to whom he was a fascinating example of Old World charm, as well as the father of a famous poet. After JBY moved into Petitpas, many of the society figures slowly receded into the background, but others continued to remain friends. They would come to his table at Petitpas and listen to the old artist expound on a great variety of subjects. He in turn would watch them and sketch his attentive audience. The Delaware Art Museum has a large number of pencil sketches by JBY that illustrate the people who frequented his lodging house. These drawings are possibly nearly all from the same sketchbook and are proof of John Sloan's remark that at Petitpas Yeats's "constant habit was to make pencil portraits."[52] Many of the Delaware sketches are of women in large hats, their heads turned as they listen to the Petitpas conversation.[53] Here Mary Shaw's hat casts a shadow over her forehead and eyes, and the artist has created a series of very heavy black pencil lines for this shaded area while the nose and chin are a series of delicate, rather hesitant lines.

Delaware Art Museum, Wilmington; Gift of Helen Farr Sloan.

32. **Dolly and John Sloan.** 1910.

49 x 35 cms. 19⅛ x 13½ inches.

Pencil on paper mounted on board.

Inscr. l.l. (in pencil in the artist's hand): "July 1910/JB Yeats."

Prov.: John Sloan.

Ref.: Murphy, illus., p. 366.

JBY first met John Sloan in 1908, but they did not become closely acquainted for another year or so. By 1910 their friendship had become quite firm, for in Sloan's diary for that year, JBY's name appears in 118 entries.[54] On July 16th, 1910, Sloan wrote, "Mr. Yeats started a portrait group in pencil of Dolly and myself in the afternoon"; this portrait is mentioned as being worked on three of the succeeding four days. On the 20th of July Yeats is reported as having said that "he'd like to try another sometime." The new group seems to have been begun without delay on July 22nd, and was completed the following day: "Mr. Yeats finished the new drawing of Dolly and me. It is much better than the first one."[55] Many of Yeats's more formal portrait drawings of his New York years lack the spontaneity and relaxed quality of his Petitpas sketches (such as nos. 31 and 33). This double portrait and the equally formal portraits of the Abbey Theatre players (nos. 35 and 36) were executed within a year of each other and exhibit close stylistic similarities: precise hatching on the faces and a noticeable degree of care in the drawing of the torsos. Despite his greater precision in drawing the full figure, Yeats was unable in the Sloan group to overcome a lifelong weakness in the drawing of hands, and there is a definite awkwardness in the way John Sloan grips his knee.

Delaware Art Museum, Wilmington; Gift of Helen Farr Sloan.

33. **Dolly Sloan.** 1910.

18.5 x 15.4 cms. 7⅛ x 5⅞ inches.

Pencil on paper.

Prov.: John Sloan.

Ref.: Murphy, illus., p. 464.

There are ten pencil drawings of Dolly Sloan in the Sloan Collection of Yeats drawings in Wilmington. No. 32 shows her in a double portrait with her husband. This one, like the other eight, is a single portrait of a woman for whom Yeats developed a great fondness. In his sketches of this outspoken woman of Catholic Irish extraction JBY conveys the obviously relaxed relationship that existed between the two friends. Here she is drawn with her elbow resting on the back of a chair or sofa, her gaze fixed on something slightly to the left of the artist. Yeats has left a greater space above the sitter's head than he usually allowed in his pencil sketches. Dolly Sloan's body is thus quite far down on the page, her head in the center of the sheet, so we are forced to concentrate on her intense stare and on the thin hatching lines of pencil that make up her face. The proximity to the sitter allows the painter far greater investigation of Dolly Sloan's strong features than did the formal distance of the double portrait.

Delaware Art Museum, Wilmington; Gift of Helen Farr Sloan.

34. **Single Tax.** c. 1910.

12.7 x 17.8 cms. 4⅞ x 6⅞ inches.

Pencil on paper.

Inscr. l.r. (in the artist's hand): "Single Tax," signed "JB Yeats."

Prov.: John Sloan.

All sorts of people came to Yeats's table at Petitpas, and the sketchbook from which this sheet has been removed has drawings of society ladies, New York writers, the Petitpas sisters, and the Sloans. This sketch is of an advocate of social and fiscal reform, a Single Taxer, though it is difficult to be certain of his identity. In July 1910 John Sloan wrote in his diary of dining at Petitpas with Yeats and there meeting a Dr. Miller, "a harsh voiced 'single taxer' who expounded Henry George trying to show how it surpassed Socialism. I admit that I couldn't see it. . . ."[56] Henry George (1839-97) was an American economist whose book *Progress and Poverty* (1879) proposed "to abolish all taxation save that upon land values," the aim being to establish equal rights in land for all and so to raise wages. The figure in the sketch cannot, obviously, be George himself, and it has so far proved impossible to discover any information on Sloan's Dr. Miller. JBY has captured his table companion in sharp profile. The sketch is very loosely drawn, yet, as is so often the case, the face and head are given a firmness that conveys character and animation.

Delaware Art Museum, Wilmington; Gift of Helen Farr Sloan.

35. **Sara Allgood.** 1911.

26.7 x 28 cms. 10⅜ x 10⅞ inches.

Pencil on paper.

Inscr.: "Sara Allgood" (in the sitter's hand) and "JB Yeats/1911" (in the artist's hand).

Prov.: Purchased by John Quinn from the artist. Later in the collection of Millicent Rogers. (Sale, Parke-Bernet, New York, April 23, 1963.)

Ref.: Murphy, pp. 390-91; illus., p. 406.

In 1911 the Abbey Theatre Company of Dublin was on a tour of the United States, and JBY was commissioned by John Quinn to do drawings of eight of the players (see also no. 36). Sara Allgood (1883-1950) was a leading actress in the company and originated the role of the Widow Quin in Synge's *The Playboy of the Western World* (1907). JBY had known the sitter in Dublin and in the past had spoken ambiguously of her abilities as an actress, noticing that her fiery performances were popular because the Irish people understood "oratory not poetry."[57] This side-view portrait concentrates on the face of the actress. The hatching is extremely closely handled.

Collection of Mr. and Mrs. J. Robert Maguire.

36. **Udolphus (Dossie) Wright.** 1911.

28 x 26.7 cms. 10⅞ x 10⅜ inches.

Pencil on paper.

Inscr. (in pencil in the artist's hand): "JB Yeats/Decr 1911."

Prov.: Purchased by John Quinn from the artist. Later in the collection of Millicent Rogers. (Sale, Parke-Bernet, New York, April 23, 1963.)

Ref.: Murphy, pp. 390-91, 405; illus., p. 406.

Both Wright and Sara Allgood (no. 35) were actors with the Abbey Theatre on their American tour in 1911. Under commission from John Quinn, JBY's eight drawings of the Irish actors were sources of great pride to the artist. Two years after their execution the drawings appeared on a decorated Irish linen handkerchief that sold for a dollar and was part of a fund-raising campaign led by Lady Gregory to help build a museum of modern art in Dublin,[58] a project that eventually had to be abandoned.

Collection of Mr. and Mrs. J. Robert Maguire.

37. **Jeanne Robert Foster.** 1917.

35.5 x 42.5 cms. 13¾ x 16⅝ inches.

Pencil on paper.

Inscr. l.r. (in the artist's hand): "JB Yeats/1917."

Prov.: From the sitter to William M. Murphy.

Ref.: Murphy, illus., p. 469.

JBY met Jeanne Robert Foster in 1911 when she was assistant editor of the *Review of Reviews*, a New York journal edited by Albert Shaw.[59] They soon became close friends, and she took care of the artist in his final days. This and other sketches of Mrs. Foster were made in 1917 in preparation for a large oil that was never begun.[60] Mrs. Foster also acquired a number of JBY's Irish paintings and drawings from John Quinn's estate.

In this drawing JBY has reverted to the Whistler-like image which he had first tried some two decades earlier (see nos. 19, 22, and 23), of a woman alone, relaxing in a chair. Unlike the drawings of the turn of the century, which are largely three-quarter length, the drawing of Mrs. Foster, like that of Dolly Sloan (no. 33), is a head and shoulder study that brings us close to the subject. We are brought directly to the face and are spared the distractions of limbs or opened books. We can thus study the fascinating clarity of the sitter's features: her staring eyes, broad mouth, and strong chin. The finials of the chair conveniently frame her tilted head, and their solidity firmly plants the figure in space.

Collection of William M. Murphy.

38. **Self-Portrait.** 1919.

57.2 x 72.5 cms. 22⅜ x 28⅛ inches.

Pencil on paper.

Inscr. (in the artist's hand): "Myself/seen through a/glass darkly/by/JB Yeats/Oct. 1919."

Prov.: From Jeanne Robert Foster to William M. Murphy.

Ref.: Denis Donoghue, "John Butler Yeats," in *Abroad in America: Visitors to the New Nation, 1776-1914*, ed. Marc Pachter and Frances Wein (Washington, D.C.: National Portrait Gallery, 1976), p. 260; Murphy, illus., pp. 449, 384ff.; Judith Zilczer, *"The Noble Buyer": John Quinn, Patron of the Avant-Garde* (Washington, D.C.: Smithsonian Institution, 1978), p. 191 (where it is erroneously described as an oil).

Exh.: National Portrait Gallery, Washington, D.C., 1976; *Abroad in America*, p. 256.

In February 1911 John Quinn commissioned an oil self-portrait from JBY. The artist was to become obsessed with the oil over the next eleven years and to leave it unfinished on his death in 1922. During his early experiments on the project JBY worked at John Sloan's studio, but it took him so long to get started, even to lift a brush, that he soon drove Sloan mad with impatience. In May 1911 he moved the canvas and pencil sketches to his room at Petitpas, a dark, one-windowed bedroom that for the next decade was to serve as both home and studio. Originally the self-portrait was to be only a head and shoulders,[61] but it slowly took on a life of its own, and within a short time Yeats was working on a three-quarter-length portrait of himself standing in his bedroom, a bookcase behind him and paint cans and brushes in the foreground.[62] Yeats sketched and resketched himself during the eleven years that went into the making of the oil self-portrait. Although Quinn was awaiting the finished oil, he supplemented the artist's income by occasionally ordering separate self-portrait sketches, and it is possible that the exhibited sketch is part of a commission of around July 1919 for two drawings for which Yeats was paid $25 each.[63] In these drawings the artist would occasionally change the positioning of his hands, but, always dressed in a black three-piece suit, a loose high collar, and broad tie, he looks intently at the spectator. The artist drew himself from a mirror, often complaining of the insufficient light in the small room. The drawings are usually devoid of background detail and, as in the exhibited sketch, show the old man with a pencil in hand, at least half his body covered by generous shadows that were a result of his having to stand with his

myself
Seen through the
glass darkly
by
JB Yeats
Oct. 1909.

back to the light so as to face the mirror. As the inscription tells us, this is JBY "seen through a glass darkly."[64]

During the 1910s JBY frequently wrote to his son Jack informing him of the progress of the self-portrait and of his rather restricted conditions: "From where my small mirror is placed my face has to be painted with a good deal of shadow on it, which as you know adds greatly to the difficulty."[65] Later he writes, "I am forced to stand close to the canvas, and also to the mirror, and though this increases the difficulty it adds immensely to the value of the practice."[66] While working on the self-portrait, JBY made occasional visits to the Metropolitan Museum of Art in New York City, and in 1917, writing to Dolly Sloan, he praised the magnificent Rembrandts: "Quantities of faces in deep obscurity and all modelled to the last degree. In all other artists including Whistler, the modelling disappears when the face is in shadow—no one but Rembrandt could model faces in shadow."[67] JBY took great comfort in the knowledge that the great masters had worked "incessantly" on self-portraiture. Rembrandt, he wrote to Jack, did not trouble himself "about the likeness" but more about "the tricks of light and shade and the rendering of costume." Self-portraiture, he tells his son, "is the finest art training in the world," and advises him to begin his own soon, ending his letter by asking, "Have you got a big mirror?"![68]

On looking at the Rembrandts in the Metropolitan Museum JBY may have become acquainted with the 1660 **Self Portrait**, which had then recently come into the collection.[69] The right side of Rembrandt's face is modelled in shadow, and there is the artist's usual penetrating stare. JBY has also modelled his face in shadow, which can be read as a direct result of his cramped studio but also as an attempt to capture Rembrandt's "tricks of light and shade." The rather tired, tight-lipped expression on Rembrandt contrasts with the look of alertness on JBY's face. The necessary element of self-inquiry that affects any self-portrait is increased in JBY's case by the large number of drawings and the long period of time that went into the creation of the final portrait. The New York years are also remarkable for the hundreds of letters that JBY wrote to his family and friends in Ireland. The incessant self-expression in these letters and in the drawings gave Yeats the opportunity to reassert his existence and his independence. "I think a man," he wrote, "is never so solitary as when he stands full length before a looking glass."[70] In his solitariness we are offered, by means of the self-portrait, an affirmation of the honesty and intellectual force that is central to John Butler Yeats's view of art. This redeclaration of presence is given an added fillip when we turn to a letter written to

Jack Yeats in 1919, the year of the drawing here exhibited, in which JBY writes in his eternally optimistic fashion that his self-portrait "will be a great success. . . . I want it to make all Quinn's other portraits look out of countenance, even John's portrait of Quinn."[71] In 1909 Augustus John had painted a portrait of Quinn titled **The Man from New York**; JBY considered it "wonderfully fine," but his own portrait, he claimed, would surely beat that of the English virtuoso—"when you get it," he told Quinn "and it is hung on your walls it will have a stark reality that will outweigh all the other portraits."[72] One cannot help admiring the extraordinary stamina of this septuagenarian artist who in the face of a whole new generation of artists was ready to take up a most daunting challenge. Unfortunately the oil **Self-Portrait** never got onto Quinn's wall to be compared with the John or any other of Quinn's impressive array of paintings. After JBY's death in 1922 Quinn shipped it to Ireland, where it was to hang in the home of the artist's son W. B. Yeats and, later, of his grandson Michael Yeats.

Collection of William M. Murphy.

Notes to Catalogue

Note: All transcripts of unpublished letters, unless otherwise noted, are by William M. Murphy; quotations are from the typescripts in his possession.

1 Unpublished letter from JBY to Edward Dowden, 17 May 1868; Collection of Trinity College, Dublin.

2 Unpublished letter from JBY to Edwin Ellis, 27 August 1868; Collection of Michael Yeats.

3 *Ibid.*

4 Unpublished letter from JBY to Edward Dowden, 22 September 1870; Collection of Trinity College, Dublin.

5 See Virginia Surtees, *The Paintings and Drawings of Dante Gabriel Rossetti (1828-1882), A Catalogue Raisonne*, 2 vols. (Oxford: Clarendon Press, 1971). See plates 400 and 424-429, vol. 2.

6 In an unpublished letter of 6 February 1873 to his wife, JBY wrote: "I have ordered a frame for Aunt Gracie's portrait—a splendid one." JBY submitted the portrait to the Royal Academy but it was rejected. See Murphy, p. 105.

7 The Yeats family lived there from 1874-1878.

8 In June 1876, Jane Grace Yeats, the artist's sixth child, died. It is possible that this sketch was made on a bereavement envelope dating from around that time.

9 "She had always, my father would say, intensity," wrote WBY in "Reveries Over Childhood and Youth," *Autobiographies* (1961), p. 62, "and that was his chief word of praise."

10 P. 82.

11 Dublin Sketching Club, *Annual Exhibition of Sketches, Pictures and Photography*..., The Leinster Hall, 35 Molesworth St., ...A Loan Collection of Pictures by Mr. Whistler is also on view. ([December] 1884). See also Andrew McLaren Young, Margaret MacDonald, Robin Spencer with Hamish Miles, *The Paintings of James McNeill Whistler* (New Haven and London: Yale University Press, 1980), 2 vols.; vol. 1, p. 60; and Ronald Anderson, "Whistler in Dublin, 1884," *Irish Arts Review*, vol. 3, Autumn 1986, pp. 45-51.

12 *Autobiographies*, pp. 82-83.

13 The man in the center of this trio is possibly John F. Taylor, Q.C., a prominent barrister; see JBY's sketch of him in Murphy, p. 143.

14 P. 140.

15 Many of the sketches are now in the National Gallery of Ireland. See *National Gallery of Ireland, Illustrated Summary Catalogue of Drawings, Watercolours and Miniatures* (Dublin: National Gallery of Ireland, 1983), nos. 6078-6083 and 7357-7365.

16 D.J. Gordon, *W.B. Yeats: Images of a Poet* (Manchester, England: Manchester University Press, 1970), p. 8.

17 The original drawing is lost. The reproduction appears in *Leisure Hour*, vol. 36, 1887, p. 637 (wood-engraving by R. Taylor).

18 26 May 1924; quoted in Allan Wade (ed.), *The Letters of W.B. Yeats* (London: Rupert Hart-Davis, 1954), p. 705.

19 See James Thorpe, *English Illustration: the Nineties* (London: Hacker Art Books, 1975), p. 10.

20 Hone, p. 61. The source of his subjects is not known. Some years earlier, in 1888, in order to raise much needed money, JBY had decided to write a ghost story which he planned to illustrate. He dictated the story to his daughter Lollie, but it failed to sell (see Murphy, p. 159).

21 London, Dent, 1895.

22 The sketchbook is one of many in the collection of the artist's granddaughter. This one has 36 leaves, of which these examples are nos. 34 and 35; the inside cover carries the inscription: "JB Yeats/3 Blenheim Rd./Bedford Pk./W."

23 See in particular his work in Jean Ingelow's *Poems* (1866). A reproduction appears in Forrest Reid's *Illustrations of the Eighteen Sixties* (London: Dover, 1975), fig. 9.

24 See K. McConkey, "The Bouguereau of the Naturalists: Bastien-Lepage and British Art," *Art History*, vol. 1, no. 3 (September 1978), pp. 371-82; also Simon Watney, *English Post-Impressionism* (London: Trefoil Books, 1980).

25 One oil painting of this period, **The Bird Market** (Hugh Lane Municipal Gallery of Modern Art, Dublin) (Fig. 9), dating from the mid-1880s, although not set in a landscape, can be seen as an example of Yeats's experimenting in the then current realist trend. The brush work is smooth and the forms are built up by means of tone rather than color.

26 Simon Watney, *op. cit.*, p. 14; Stevenson's ideas appeared in *Velázquez* (London, 1899).

27 *A Loan Collection of Pictures by Nathaniel Hone RHA, and John Butler Yeats RHA*, October-November, 1901, at 6 St Stephen's Green, Dublin; p. 10.

28 Hone, p. 57. In 1901 Sarah Purser (1848-1943), a Dublin portrait painter, organized the Nathaniel Hone-JBY exhibition in Dublin, the only comprehensive exhibition of their works that either artist was to enjoy in his lifetime.

29 Murphy, p. 185. For a fuller discussion of this drawing see the accompanying essay.

30 Murphy, p. 207.

31 Simon Watney, *op. cit.*, p. 13.

32 Reproduced in the exhibition catalogue *Fantin-Latour* (Ottawa: National Gallery of Canada, 1983), no. 42, p. 142.

33 P. 137.

34 "John Butler Yeats RHA," *The Dublin Magazine*, no. 1 (January 1924), p. 483.

35 Murphy, p. 225.

36 JBY, "Watts and the Method of Art," *Essays Irish and American* (1918), p. 79. See also Murphy's essay herein, pp. 13-14.

37 See Murphy, illus., p. 141.

38 Judith Zilczer, *"The Noble Buyer": John Quinn, Patron of the Avant-Garde*, Hirshhorn Museum and Sculpture Garden, Smithsonian Institution, Washington, D.C. (1978), p. 191. It is worth mentioning that Moore as a young man in Paris had been painted by Manet, Blanche, Degas and Sickert; for a list of portraits of Moore, see Robert Becker, "Artists Look at George Moore," *Irish Arts Review*, vol. 2, no. 4 (Winter, 1985), pp. 56-65. JBY's oil portrait of Moore (unfinished) is in the National Gallery of Ireland, Dublin. The best work on Quinn is B.L. Reid, *The Man from New York* (New York: Oxford, 1968). See also Murphy, *Prodigal Father*.

39 E.J.G., "Loan Exhibition of Paintings by Mr. Hone RHA and Mr. Yeats RHA," *The Irish Times*, 21 October 1901.

40 Murphy, p. 286.

41 Unpublished letter from JBY to John Quinn, 14 March 1911: part of the Jeanne R. Foster-William M. Murphy Collection of the New York Public Library.

42 Murphy, p. 323.

43 Hone, p. 90.

44 There is an oil of 1903 in the National Gallery of Ireland and drawings in Sligo County Library and Museum, Sligo, and in the collection of the Abbey Theatre, Dublin.

45 Augusta Lady Gregory, *Sir Hugh Lane, His Life and Legacy* (Colin Smythe: Gerrard's Cross, Buckinghamshire, 1973), p. 45.

46 A noticeable exception is the splendid sketch of Synge now in the National Gallery of Ireland.

47 Murphy, pp. 248ff.

48 A similar sketch is in the Delaware Art Museum (the gift of Helen Farr Sloan), where the man is on the left and the sketch is inscribed "The Mademoiselles Petitpas"; see Murphy, illus., p. 353.

49 The oil is of 1920. Writing to Lily, his daughter, JBY pronounced it "a masterpiece: a life size portrait of her sitting in her chair" (Hone, p. 272).

50 Murphy, pp. 354f.

51 Pp. 287, 353.

52 Bruce St. John, ed., *John Sloan's New York Scene* (New York: Harper and Row, 1965), p. 367.

53 "It is sometimes amusing at dinner," wrote JBY to his son Jack, "to watch the people and their style of hats" (unpublished letter of 31 March 1916). Collection of Anne Yeats.

54 Murphy, pp. 359-60 and 367.

55 *John Sloan's New York Scene, op. cit.*, p. 441.

56 P. 439.

57 Murphy, p. 298.

58 Pp. 391 and 406.

59 P. 395.

60 P. 468.

61 A head and shoulders was painted for Quinn and is now in the Sligo County Library and Museum, Sligo; see Judith Zilczer, *op. cit.*, p. 20 and pp. 191-192.

62 See Murphy, color illus., frontispiece. The painting is now in the collection of the artist's grandson, Michael Butler Yeats.

63 Murphy, p. 494.

64 This is of course based on the passage from the first Epistle of Paul to the Corinthians, xiii, 12-13: "When I became a man I put away childish things. For now we see through a glass, darkly; but then face to face: now I know in part; but then shall I know even as also I am known."

65 Unpublished letter of 19 May 1914. Collection of Anne Yeats.

66 Unpublished letter of 4 January 1919. Collection of Anne Yeats.

67 Unpublished letter of 17 May 1917. Collection of Princeton University.

68 Unpublished letter of 7 March 1916. Collection of Anne Yeats.

69 Bequest of Benjamin Altman, 1913.

70 Lennox Robinson (ed.), *Further Letters of John Butler Yeats* (Dublin: Cuala, 1920), p. 56; the letter dates from 1919.

71 Unpublished letter of 5 February 1919. Collection of Anne Yeats.

72 Hone, p. 130, letter no. 77, and p. 260, letter no. 210. The John portrait is now owned by the Astor, Lenox and Tilden Foundation and is on loan to the New York Public Library. See Judith Zilczer, *op. cit.*, p. 163.

Bibliography

Archibald, Douglas. *John Butler Yeats.* Lewisburg, Pa.: Bucknell University Press, 1974.

Arnold, Bruce. *Orpen.* London: J. Cape, 1981.

Barrett, Cyril. *Irish Art in the Nineteenth Century: An Exhibition of Irish Victorian Art at Crawford Municipal School of Art.* Cork, 1971.

Bodkin, Thomas. "John Butler Yeats RHA" *The Dublin Magazine* 1 (January 1924), No. 6: 478-87.

Brooks, Van Wyck. *John Sloan, A Painter's Life.* New York: Dutton, 1955.

Campbell, Julian. *The Irish Impressionists, Irish Artists in France and Belgium, 1850-1914.* Dublin: National Gallery of Ireland, 1984.

Cooper, Douglas. *The Courtauld Collection, A Catalogue and Introduction.* London: University of London, Athlone Press, 1954.

Crookshank, Anne, and the Knight of Glin. *Painters of Ireland, c. 1660-1920.* London: Barrie and Jenkins, 1978.

Cross, T. A. Introduction to *The Slade Tradition, 1871-1971, A Centenary Contribution.* London: The Fine Arts Society, 1971.

Curry, D. Park. *James McNeill Whistler at the Freer Gallery of Art.* Washington, D. C.: Freer Gallery of Art, 1984.

Donoghue, Denis, "John Butler Yeats," in *Abroad in America: Visitors to the New Nation, 1776-1914,* ed. Marc Pachter and Frances Wein (Washington, D.C.: National Portrait Gallery, 1976), p. 260.

Druick, Douglas, and Michel Hoog. *Fantin-Latour.* Exhibition Catalogue. Ottawa: National Gallery of Canada, 1983.

Elzea, Betty. *Frederick Sandys.* Exhibition Catalogue. Brighton, England: Brighton Museum and Art Gallery, 1974.

Flint, Kate, ed. *Impressionists in England: The Critical Reception.* Boston: Routledge and Kegan Paul, 1984.

Getscher, Robert H. *The Stamp of Whistler.* Exhibition Catalogue. Oberlin, Ohio: Oberlin College, 1977.

Glazebrook, Mark, ed. *Artists and Architecture of Bedford Park: 1875-1900.* London: Shenval Press, 1967.

Gordon, Donald James. *W. B. Yeats, Images of a Poet.* Manchester, England: Manchester University Press, 1961.

Gordon, Robert. *John Butler Yeats and John Sloan: The Records of a Friendship.* Dublin: Dolmen, 1978.

Houfe, Simon. *The Dictionary of British Book Illustrators and Caricaturists (1800-1914).* Ithaca: Antique Collectors Club, 1978.

House, John. *Impressionism, Its Masters, Its Precursors, and Its Influence in Britain.* London: Royal Academy of Arts, 1974.

Laughton, Bruce. Introduction to *The Slade (1871-1971), A Centenary Exhibition.* London: Royal Academy of Arts, 1971.

Laughton, Bruce. *Philip Wilson Steer, 1860-1942.* Oxford: Clarendon Press, 1971.

Lochnan, Katherine K. *The Etchings of James McNeill Whistler.* London and New Haven: Yale University Press, 1984.

Muir, Percival Horace. *Victorian Illustrated Books.* London: Batsford, 1971.

Murphy, William M. *Prodigal Father: The Life of John Butler Yeats (1839-1922).* Ithaca and London: Cornell University Press, 1978.

Murphy, William M. *The Yeats Family and the Pollexfens of Sligo.* Dublin: Dolmen, 1971.

Pyle, Hilary. *Jack B. Yeats: A Biography.* London: Routledge and Kegan Paul, 1970.

Reid, Benjamin Lawrence. *The Man from New York: John Quinn and His Friends.* New York: Oxford University Press, 1968.

Reid, Forrest. *Illustrators of the Eighteen Sixties.* New York: Dover, 1975.

St. John, Bruce, ed. *John Sloan's New York Scene, From the Diaries, Notes and Correspondence, 1906-1913.* New York: Harper and Row, 1965.

Stevenson, R. A. M. *Velázquez (1899).* Rev. ed. by Thomas Crombie and Denys Sutton. London: G. Bell, 1962.

Thorpe, James. *English Illustration: The Nineties.* London: Hacker Art Books, 1975.

Watney, Simon. *English Post-Impressionism.* London: Trefoil Books, 1980.

White, James. *John Butler Yeats and the Irish Renaissance.* Dublin: Dolmen, 1972.

Yeats, John Butler. *Essays Irish and American.* Dublin: Talbot Press, 1918; London: T. F. Unwin, Ltd. 1918.

Yeats, John Butler. *Further Letters of John Butler Yeats.* Edited by Lennox Robinson. Churchtown, Dundrum: The Cuala Press, 1920.

Yeats, John Butler. *John Butler Yeats, Letters to His Son William Butler Yeats and Others.* Edited by Joseph Hone. Preface by Oliver Elton. New York: E. P. Dutton, 1946.

Yeats, John Butler. *Passages from the Letters of J. B. Yeats.* Edited by Ezra Pound. Churchtown, Dundrum: The Cuala Press, 1917.

Yeats, William Butler. *Autobiographies.* London: Macmillan, 1956; 1961.

Zilczer, Judith. *"The Noble Buyer": John Quinn, Patron of the Avant-Garde.* Washington, D. C.: Smithsonian Institution Press, 1978.